YOU'RE GOING TO
SURVIVE

True stories from people who've endured

soul-crushing moments in their careers—failure,

rejection, disappointment, public humiliation—

and how they got through it,

and how you will too.

ALEXANDRA FRANZEN

You're Going to Survive: True stories from people who've endured soul-
crushing moments in their careers—failure, rejection, disappointment,
public humiliation—and how they got through it, and how you will too.

Library of Congress Cataloging-in-Publication number: 2017915546.
ISBN: (paperback) 978-1-63353-679-1, (ebook) 978-1-63353-680-7
BISAC category code SEL027000 SELF-HELP / Personal Growth /
Success

Printed in the United States of America

Praise

"This book is your new best friend on a bad day. Keep it by your bedside table, in your dashboard, in your purse, or in your freezer next to a big pint of ice cream. Alexandra will always be there to tell you that you can do it, you must keep going, and you are meant for greatness."

—Vanessa Van Edwards, *Entrepreneur* columnist and bestselling author of *Captivate: The Science of Succeeding with People*

"No matter what you're going through, you're not alone! This collection of stories will help you find the courage, focus, and traction to take the next steps toward brilliance in your life and career."

—Todd Henry, author of *The Accidental Creative and Die Empty*

"**You're Going to Survive** is a must-read book for anyone with an ambitious career dream. Alexandra's writing is encouraging, comforting, and uplifting, with just the right amount of get-up-and-do-it motivation."

—Liz Dennery Sanders, Brand Consultant, Creative Director, founder of SheBrand

"Making art is my thing. Putting it out into the world is not. Even after showing my work hundreds of times, I still have moments when I feel uneasy, discouraged, and defeated. In those moments, this book is like a shot of caffeine to the soul. The stories in **You're Going to Survive** make me stand up straight and feel braver, energized, and ready to run strong and steady to the next challenge."

—Kent Youngstrom, Painter

"*You're Going to Survive* will strengthen your spirit when things aren't going 'exactly as planned' in your career. Everyone goes through tough times, and sometimes the 'small stuff' feels like 'big stuff,' but you don't have to feel alone. Enjoy this witty and insightful read!"

—Kristine Carlson, coauthor of the *Don't Sweat the Small Stuff* book series

"Alexandra sets the standard for how I hope to show up in the world as a writer, a creative, a teacher, and a human. Everything she shares oozes with conscientiousness and intimate care. *You're Going to Survive* stands out as a paradigm-shifting work that you'll hold in your heart, as I do, with a permanent sense of gratitude. This book is so fluid, uplifting, and earnest that you may find yourself reading it ten times over—especially in a dark, unkind, or sticky stretch."

—Dave Ursillo, author of *Big Apple, Black Sand and the Midnight Sun* and *Lead Without Followers*

"When life challenges us—and it will—we need support, balm for the weary disappointment. Alex is here to offer us that. Hearing how others have overcome reminds us that we aren't alone and that yes, we are going to survive."

—Carrie-Anne Moss, Actress (*The Matrix* trilogy, *Memento*, *Chocolat*, *Jessica Jones*) and founder of Annapurna Living

"Alexandra has a true gift for making the hardest things in life feel infinitely easier. *You're Going to Survive* isn't just a playbook for getting through tough situations—it's ray after inspiring ray of sunshine for anyone going through a dark time. As a writer, an entrepreneur, and a human, I'll turn to this book for encouragement again and again."

—Adrian Granzella Larssen, Editor-at-Large, *The Muse*

"Alexandra Franzen is like a cool big sister who's got your back, with the kind of humor and honesty that will make you feel less alone and more motivated to keep going when chasing your dream gets tough (we're talking client-from-hell, one-star-review, oh-my-God-what-am-I-even-doing tough). Every creative needs this book on their nightstand for those inevitable bad days."

—Kathleen Shannon, host of the *Being Boss Podcast*, cofounder of Braid Creative

"If you want to follow your dreams, at some point you are going to have to step up, put yourself out there, try new things, and take risks. And when you do that, you can be pretty sure that some things won't work out. When that happens, instead of giving up on your dreams, open this book. *You're Going to Survive* will get you back on track, find the gold in what just happened, and help you focus on what really matters. Alexandra's laser-sharp insight and comforting humor will convince you that not only will you survive, you will thrive."

—Beth Kempton, author of *Freedom Seeker* and founder of Do What You Love

"It's one thing to say *'Never give up!'* but it's another thing to actually live through the pain of rejection and disappointment that makes you question your work and your worth. When that happens, read this book. It will get you through."

—Nicole Antoinette, host of *Real Talk Radio*

"Seriously—I couldn't put this book down! Every story in **You're Going to Survive** is filled with 'aha!' moments, honest reflections, and raw stories from people who faced defeat, but mustered through to survive. If you find yourself having an existential crisis every few months and often wonder *'WTF am I doing with my life?'* then this book is just the pick-me-up you need. It takes you from down in the dumps to 'I am going to survive and I can do this' after just one story.

—Lindsey Smith, public speaker and author of *Eat Your Feelings: The Food Mood Girl's Guide to Transforming Your Emotional Eating*

"Whether you're a social worker (my previous career) or an artist (my current career) every profession includes beauty—and plenty of challenges, too. **You're Going to Survive** is a book that reminds readers: not only are you strong enough to navigate the ups and downs of your career path, but your mistakes, disappointments, and setbacks can be a wide-open canvas where beauty and possibility emerge."

—Kelly Rae Roberts, artist and author of *Taking Flight: Inspiration and Techniques to Give Your Creative Spirit Wings*

"This book is a gem. I have no idea how Alexandra convinced so many incredible, accomplished people to reveal their most cringeworthy examples of career failure, but I'm incredibly grateful that she did. ***You're Going to Survive*** feels like the best friend who listens patiently to the story of your worst ever day at work and then tells you exactly what you needed to hear to bust out of your funk, reclaim your mojo, and get back to kicking butt. This book is perfect for those disastrous days at work when you really, really need to be reminded that you're not alone, and that you don't suck. You will get through this and you will bounce back."

—Jo Miller, Founding Editor of *Be Leaderly*

"If you ever think to yourself, *'Why am I even bothering to keep trying to do what I care about?'* then this book is for you. And me. And all of us. We need reminders from people who have been there that ebb and flow is the nature of life and work, not a sign that there is something uniquely wrong with us when things don't go as planned. This book is that reminder."

—Anna Guest-Jelley, founder of Curvy Yoga, as seen in *The New York Times*, *The Washington Post*, and *xoJane*

"A writer, a teacher, a guide, a muse: whatever Alexandra Franzen does, she does it with a mission of kindness, love, and acceptance. I don't think anyone could better navigate the lowest lows with such wisdom, humor and strength. There's nobody else I'd want as my survival skills guide."

—Michelle Ward, Career Coach, as seen in *New York Magazine*, *The Huffington Post*, and *Newsweek*

Foreword

By Sarah Von Bargen.
Founder of Yes & Yes.

It's fall of 2010 and, between sips of lukewarm coffee, I discover that I've inadvertently achieved the Holy Grail Of Blogging: something I've written has gone viral.

And what's more, something I've written has gone viral via Reddit, that usually-cantankerous-quick-to-criticize online forum.

I watch with wonder as new comments and readers pour into my site. I refresh Reddit and see my article—"31 Things I've Learned in 31 Years"—work its way up the page.

And then the first snarky comment lands in my inbox.

"This isn't wise. Anybody with half a brain has learned these things before they leave high school."

My inbox pings again. As the day progresses, I'm told that I write like a teenager and that I look ten years older than I am. Commenters tell me I should keep my day job (I wasn't planning on leaving it) and that I used the wrong form of 'compliment' (I didn't).

A day that started with rose-colored glasses and visions of a book deal ends in tears. I eat my feelings and consider deleting my entire blog.

Instead I called Alexandra.

Alex Franzen, the author of the book you're holding right this second, is my IRL friend and perhaps the world's best pep-talk giver. You see, she doesn't just give pep talks via books. She also gives them to her friends, in real life, after trolls say that said friend is *"collectively lowering the IQ of the Internet."*

Good friend that she is, Alex was able to raise my spirits and give me a loving reality check. She assured me that, regardless of the trolls and the traffic spike of meanies, I'd survive. I'd live to blog another day! She reminded me that I could choose to gather myself up, brush myself off, and keep writing, blogging, and publishing.

She was right, of course. In the years since that post went viral, I've encountered other setbacks, trolls, and snark— online and off. And you know what? I've survived all of those as well.

Maybe you've never been trolled online, but I'm sure you've encountered your own version of this. You've been passed over for a promotion, dumped, or fired. Maybe your application wasn't accepted. Perhaps you showed up for picture day with a stain on your shirt, a giant zit, and greasy hair.

Whatever the setback, this book (and Alex) will help.

Dedication

This book is dedicated to Suzanna. You are a survivor, in a million different ways, and one of the strongest people I've ever met. I can't wait to watch you rise into the next chapter of your life—and career.

Having a Rough Day at Work? Worried About Your Career? Feeling Frustrated? Overwhelmed? Embarrassed? Discouraged?

You are *definitely* not alone.

Right this second, somewhere in the world, I can guarantee:

—There's a graphic designer who's wondering how he's going to find enough clients to pay his rent this month.

—There's a restaurant owner who just peeked at Yelp and noticed yet another one-star review—and it's four paragraphs long and filled with angry exclamation points. Yikes.

—There's a Senator who's panicking that she might disappoint her constituents, that she won't get re-elected, or that an unflattering photo will get posted online and the Internet goblins will mock her clothes, her hair, and her beliefs.

Everywhere, in every corner of every city, and in every industry and profession, everyone's going through... *something*.

Everyone's grappling with some kind of challenge. It might be a huge challenge, or a comparatively small one. It might be happening privately, or publicly, or even on live TV. But everyone's dealing with *something*, and everyone has moments where they wonder, *"Am I going to make it?" "Why are people so cruel?" "Do I have what it takes to excel in my industry?" "Am I stupid for even attempting this project/path/semi-crazy idea?" "Why does it feel like my career is a flaming dumpster fire?" "Will it ever get easier?" "Maybe I should quit and begin a new life in a nunnery?"*

I've felt that way many times. The person sitting in the cubicle or coffee shop seat next to yours—they've felt that way, too.

I wrote this book because I wanted to remind people (including myself) that feeling frustrated, discouraged, criticized, and rejected in the course of your career is actually...*very normal.*

Every career has its ups and downs. Everyone goes through dry spells, difficulties, and setbacks at some point or another—even A-list celebrities and presidential nominees. We're all striving and struggling together.

Whatever you're going through right now, or whatever you're worrying might happen next, I want you to know: *You're going to survive.*

Yeah, you might cry. Sure, you might feel compelled to eat an entire family-sized pizza all by yourself. Of course, you might want to crawl under a blanket and self-medicate with Netflix for the entire weekend because you're a human being with human feelings and sometimes things *hurt.*

But no matter what happens, you're going to survive. The silver lining is that you'll become a smarter, wiser, funnier, more compassionate person because of whatever you've endured in your life and career. Like they say, "pressure creates diamonds." It may not always feel like it, but sometimes, the worst moment of your entire career can be the catalyst for a new chapter, a new project, a brilliant new invention or system—maybe the best work you've ever done.

* * *

HI. HAVE WE MET?

It's probably a good idea for me to introduce myself, in case we've never met...

Hello! My name is Alexandra Franzen, but most people call me "Alex." I also respond to "Ali," "Al," "Franz," and "Hey, you with the blue hair."

For most of my grown-up life, I've worked as a writer, editor, and communication consultant. I've also worked in the public broadcasting industry, which you'll read about later in this book. And one time, I helped my sweetheart Brandon open a brunch restaurant. You'll read a few stories about that, too.

But for the last eight years or so, writing has been my main gig. I've been blessed with truly incredible clients over the years, exciting publishing and teaching opportunities, and a few projects that have literally caused me to erupt into tears of gratitude and joy.

(Spoiler alert: I'm a crier and a hugger. I cry a lot. Sometimes while hugging people.)

Throughout my career, there have been beautiful *"I can't believe this is really my job, somebody pinch me"* moments. And also…moments that were not so exuberant. Difficult moments. Embarrassing moments. Bewildering moments—like having my identity stolen and seeing a fake website that someone created, pretending to be me, passing my work—and my personal stories—off as their own. There's been rejection, criticism, and just about every flavor of discouragement that you can imagine.

After my first book came out, here's one of the reviews that got posted on Amazon:

"Awful. I thought these would be cute, preprinted notes that I could send to friends. But each one uses the word 'Awesome' in some over-the-top, silly way. I am a grown woman who enjoys sending encouraging notes to my friends, but these are very juvenile (think pre-teen). I wish I could return them. Unless you are 8–12, don't buy these."

Ouch.

After my next book came out—this time, a self-published novel that was very, very loosely based on my real life—here's what one reader had to say:

"Did not finish due to the main character being so unlikeable [. . .] The writing is mediocre with nothing but excessive commas, especially where they're

19

*redundant and never should have been considered
[. . .] I guess I shouldn't have expected much from
the writing."*

Yikes.

And then there's another book project I worked on—a
journal with daily questions for couples to answer
together. I loved this project and I was so proud of how
it turned out. It ended up being a number one bestseller,
multiple years running. But, uh, not everyone loved it.
Here's one review:

*"Questions are boring. I expected this to have some
depth to it."*

Ouch again.

When I see negative reviews about my work, it stings.
I wish I could say, *"It doesn't bother me at all—not
even for one single second—because my confidence is
unshakable and I am sooo brave!"* but that just isn't
true. The truth is that...*it hurts.*

If you're a chef and someone spits out your food, that's
not fun to witness.

If you're a writer and someone posts a one-star review
about your latest art project, that's not much fun either.

And also, let's be honest...it's not fun when you're job-
hunting and you apply for ten different positions and
don't get a single response.

It's not fun when you submit a completed project to a client, and they hate every single part of it, and you have to do the entire thing all over again from scratch.

It's not fun when you watch your colleague get chosen for a promotion that you wanted (even though you're more qualified and everyone knows it, so seriously, WTF?).

It's not fun when your book proposal gets rejected by the thirty-seventh literary agent or publisher in a row.

It's not fun when your parents disapprove of your career ambitions and think you're a delusional idiot.

And it's definitely not fun when online trolls take pleasure in ripping apart your work, purely for their own amusement.

Nobody wants this kind of stuff to happen. Most of us have nightmares about these kinds of scenarios. We try to shield ourselves from pain and disappointment. We cringe even just thinking about it. We try our darnedest to avoid these bleak situations.

But this kind of stuff...happens. It happens a lot. Our lives do not always flow along like silken tofu. Sometimes, challenges arise. Sometimes, things just... seriously suck.

And then what?

How can we survive moments like that?

How can we handle discouragement with grace and strength?

How can we roll with the inevitable ups and downs of our careers without giving up? Without curling into a ball and hiding forever?

How can we stay optimistic, motivated, and inspired to keep marching forward, even after experiencing a considerable professional setback? Seriously, *how?*

These are questions I've wondered about a lot, especially over the last seven or eight years of my life and career.

To find answers to those questions, I decided to talk to a lot of smart, funny, wise people and get their advice. Then I compiled their stories—along with a few of my own—into a Word document, which eventually became an e-book, and then later a book-book. The one you're holding in your hands.

* * *

WHEN YOU START LOSING HOPE, TRUE STORIES CAN HELP.

When I'm feeling discouraged, what helps me—more than anything else—is hearing true stories about people who have experienced a similar type of discouragement.

I like reading about what happened, how they felt, how they survived the bleakest moments, and how they got stronger.

When I read or hear those kinds of stories, I always feel better. It's like soul medicine. Like a deep, intense, eight-second-long, rocking-back-'n-forth hug. Like a pep talk from a wise mentor who really cares, even if it's someone I've never met in "real life" before.

This book is filled with those kinds of stories. I call them *Survival Stories*. You'll find Survival Stories from my own career, and from lots of other peoples' careers, too.

I hope these stories help you feel a little calmer. A little more hopeful. A little less alone.

I don't know what type of person you are, or where you live, or what kind of profession you've chosen— puppeteer, astronaut, social justice warrior, or social media strategist—or what you're trying to create, build, or achieve. But I do know this:

You are much stronger than you think. Your goals are worth pursuing. You are not alone. Everyone struggles, sometimes. Everyone makes mistakes. Everyone feels the sting of rejection. Everyone gets scared. We can be scared, together, and...

We're going to survive.

TABLE OF CONTENTS

Survival Stories

This book contains true stories about terrible bosses, unimpressed clients, vicious blog comments, disappointing product sales, manuscript rejections, embarrassing workplace mistakes, misery, discouragement, defeat, and how to get through it.

You'll find a few stories from my own life and career— plus lots of stories contributed by friends and colleagues.

All of these stories are true. This stuff really happened. All of these people survived. Each of these people offered to share their story for one reason: *because they want to help you feel better.*

(Isn't it cool that there are people out there who care about you, even though they've never met you? I think that's amazing.)

Praise＿＿＿＿＿＿＿＿＿＿＿＿＿＿＿＿＿4

Foreword＿＿＿＿＿＿＿＿＿＿＿＿＿＿＿12

Chapter One:
When You Don't Get the Job That You Wanted＿26

Chapter Two:
When Someone Writes a Terrible Review About Your Work＿＿＿＿＿＿＿＿＿＿＿＿＿＿88

Chapter Three:
When Your Boss, Client, or Customer Is Totally Disappointed＿＿＿＿＿＿＿＿＿＿＿124

Chapter Four:
When Bullies and Internet Goblins Are Ruining Your Life＿＿＿＿＿＿＿＿＿＿＿＿166

Chapter Five:
When You Feel Unimportant, Untalented, and Invisible—like Nobody Cares about You, or Your Work Doesn't Matter＿＿＿＿＿＿＿＿206

Chapter Six:
When You Feel Tired, Shlumpy, Frumpy, and Unmotivated—like Achieving Your Goal Is "Just Too Hard," or It's Going to Take "Forever"＿＿234

Chapter Seven:
Survival Toolkit＿＿＿＿＿＿＿＿＿＿268

A Few Final Thoughts＿＿＿＿＿＿＿288

Gratitude＿＿＿＿＿＿＿＿＿＿＿＿298

About The Author＿＿＿＿＿＿＿＿304

Chapter One:

When You Don't Get the Job That You Wanted

MY BEST FRIEND GOT THE JOB—NOT ME.

Story contributed by: Ben Wendel.
Grammy Award-nominated musician. Composer. Producer.

A Note from Alexandra:

On a sticky-melty-hot summer day, I was driving past a Starbucks in Portland, Oregon. My phone flashed. *Call from Ben Wendel.* I pulled into the parking lot and miraculously found a spot. For the next hour or so, I sat in my car, furiously taking notes, while Ben told me how it felt to watch his best friend get the job that he wanted, and how that experience rattled his self-esteem to the core.

Ben would never say this himself, because he's very humble, but I will tell you that he's a musical genius who's been nominated for a Grammy Award. He's won about a million different prizes and grants. He's been praised in *The New York Times* and lots of other publications. He plays numerous instruments. He's immensely talented, hardworking, and respected by his peers. He's performed with Snoop Dogg and The Artist Formerly Known As Prince, which is obviously the coolest thing ever.

In addition to being a world-renowned musician, composer, and producer, Ben also happens to be my older brother—and he's one of my number one heroes. Ben has endured so much uncertainty, discouragement,

27

and rejection in order to build a career as a full-time professional musician. He's got serious grit.

I couldn't imagine a better way to kick off this book than with a story from my big brother—the boy, then teenager, then man who taught me what it means to be a devoted, disciplined artist—and actually make a living doing what you love.

Without further ado...here is Ben's story.

* * *

Ben: This one time, right after I graduated from college, my friend Shane and I both got invited to audition to tour with Ani DiFranco. She's an incredible musician who has released more than twenty albums, and she's considered one of the greatest folk-rock singers of her generation. My friend and I both came into the audition really prepared. We both sounded great. Then...Shane got the gig and I didn't.

I remember getting the news over the phone. The tour manager called to let me know—and I felt completely crushed. It hit me in my core. I was happy for Shane— he was, and still is, one of my best friends—but I felt so disappointed. This would have been an incredible opportunity for me—touring the world, at age twenty-two, with a world-class artist like Ani. But they chose Shane and not me.

I remember thinking to myself, *"Shane is so talented, so if they want him and not me, then maybe that means*

I'm not good enough to make it as a musician." I felt so scared and ashamed.

The worst part was that later the same day I was scheduled to perform at a concert—right alongside Shane! I felt so anxious about that performance. I was happy for Shane, of course, but I didn't want to see him, let alone perform next to him, especially not that same night. It was a real low point.

To help myself feel better, I decided to write out all of my feelings. After getting off the phone with the tour manager, I felt miserable, so I grabbed a beautiful handmade notebook that had been given to me as a birthday present (ironically, it was given to me by a woman named Kali—who later became Shane's wife).

The notebook was completely blank. I turned to the first page and started to write about how I was feeling. I wrote for about forty-five minutes. I didn't censor or edit myself. I didn't worry about grammar. I just vomited everything out onto the page.

Some parts of what I wrote were really petty and jealous, other parts were gracious and generous, and other parts reflected the reality of life as a musician: that sometimes you give your best effort but still don't get what you want.

By the time I was done writing, I felt so much clearer and calmer—like I had just purged all of these toxins out of my body.

That experience happened almost twenty years ago.

Today, at age forty, I have a very different perspective on criticism than I did at age twenty-two. Back then, not getting chosen for Ani's tour felt like the end of the world. It felt like "I have no talent" and "I'm never going to succeed." But now, when something doesn't pan out the way I'd hoped, my attitude is "OK, so that project isn't happening—cool. I wonder what's going to happen instead."

Because that's how it works. When someone says "No" to you, that just means that some other opportunity is going to happen instead. Something equally great. Maybe even something better. You just never know.

For example, if I had gotten that job with Ani DiFranco's tour back when I was twenty-two, then I might not have co-founded my jazz band, Kneebody. The irony is, because of Kneebody, I've gotten to tour around the world multiple times over and also received my first Grammy nomination with them. In the end, I got my wish. I got to tour with amazing musicians and see the world. Just because it didn't happen with Ani didn't mean that it wasn't going to happen eventually. The best (and perhaps most ironic) part of all of this is my buddy Shane eventually joined Kneebody and has played alongside me all these years.

I've found that one of the best things to do when you're feeling criticized is to remind yourself that every single artist in the history of mankind has gone through some version of what you're going through, and has felt some version of what you're feeling.

It can be helpful to read rejection letters that famous authors received to remind yourself that even Oscar Wilde and Nabokov and J.K. Rowling had their share of discouragement and disappointment. Or you can watch documentaries, listen to interviews, or read biographies about your personal heroes. Or read books like this one. Those types of stories will remind you that everyone has low points, everyone hears "No" sometimes, and it doesn't mean you're untalented—it's just part of the journey of being an artist.

Choosing the artist's path means saying that you are going to permanently invite criticism, humiliation, self-doubt, and all kinds of uncomfortable feelings into your life. That's part of the deal. The vulnerability never ends. Not even once you've "made" it.

The artist's path is a brutal, humble, strange one. But we do it because we love it. And the low points can make you stronger.

I've read about monks in Tibet who pray for a life that includes suffering, because they know that true wisdom only comes through life's challenges.

That kind of perspective can make the sting of rejection feel so much easier to bear—and can even make it feel like a beautiful gift.

* * *

SURVIVAL TIP:

When you feel miserable because you didn't get the job that you wanted, take a cue from Ben: vomit all of your feelings into a journal. Keep writing until you've poured out every drop of anger, shame, anxiety, and irritation that you possibly can. Get it all out. Try to get a good night's sleep...and the next day? Move onward with your job search.

Remember that when someone says "No," this isn't the end of your career. It just means that now, you have a chance to create a different kind of opportunity for yourself. Something just as good as the job you didn't get—or maybe even better.

Thank God They Didn't Hire Me.

Ben just shared a story about that one time he really wanted to get hired for a worldwide tour with one of his favorite performers—but he didn't get chosen. His best friend got the job instead, and he felt crushed. Pretty awful.

And yet...

In the end, not getting hired turned out to be a pretty great thing. Because Ben was "stuck at home"—instead of touring around the world—he decided to co-found a jazz band called Kneebody. That band is still going strong today. They even got nominated for a Grammy Award.

Would Ben still have started Kneebody if he'd gotten hired for that tour? Maybe. Maybe not. Who knows? It's interesting to think about, isn't it? Maybe not getting hired by Ani DiFranco was one of the best things to ever happen to Ben's career.

Listening to Ben's story, I found myself remembering a very similar story from my own life. Interestingly, my story also happened when I was in my early twenties, just like Ben. Here's how it went down...

I was twenty-four years old and working at a major public broadcasting company in the Midwest. It was a job that many people envied. My boss was a powerful, influential man at the company—the head of the entire Broadcast Technology department. I was his assistant and right-hand gal.

My job was a grab-bag position that included all kinds of tasks. Managing my boss's calendar. Keeping track of our department's spending. Writing technical manuals and standard operating procedures. Working with the on-air talent to get fifteen- and thirty-second promotional spots recorded on time, and then working with the traffic department to make sure those spots got scheduled into the correct slots. And about a hundred other micro-tasks that needed to get completed every week.

My days were packed with writing assignments, project coordination, endless meetings, and avalanches of emails that all seemed to be marked "urgent." It was fast-paced and high stress, but the benefits were significant. For starters, I had a very modest—but consistent—paycheck.

I had good healthcare coverage. I got to be part of a company that was doing incredible work—producing world-class radio and podcast content that touched people's lives. That was something to be proud of. And, as long as I worked hard and aced my annual performance review, I could rise through the ranks of the company. Who knows? One day, maybe I could even have my boss's job.

On paper, my situation seemed like a dream job at a dream company. And I'm sure it was *somebody's* dream job. But it wasn't mine. The truth is...I was pretty miserable.

I was young and scared about being unemployed, so I buried my feelings and repeatedly told myself, *"I love my job, I love my job. It's winter, it's really cold and dark, that's the only reason why I'm feeling sort of depressed right now. Things will get better once it's spring. I just need to hang in there."*

That's what I told myself...but it just wasn't true.

The truth, which I was terrified to admit to myself, is that I was gradually beginning to realize that I didn't want a nine-to-five job. I didn't want to work in cubicle, then a small office, then a bigger office with a window facing the parking lot. I didn't want to climb up the ladder for the next forty years and then retire. I didn't want that life. However, I didn't know what else I'd rather be doing. I didn't have a clear "exit strategy" for what I could with my career if I left my current job. I had...zero ideas. So I stayed put.

Then the Great Recession kicked in. The economy buckled. Society panicked. Everyone whispered about "funding cuts" and other scary possibilities. Suddenly, tons of my co-workers started getting laid off. People with kids, aging parents, and mortgages, losing jobs they'd had for ten or twenty years. It was terrifying.

But I had a secret, shameful fantasy that I couldn't admit to anybody...

I hoped they'd pick me next.

I know it sounds insane, but for me, at that point in my life, getting laid off sounded like...*freedom*. A fresh start. A second chance. A way to reboot my career and do something different. Something that really excited me.

Of course, I felt incredibly guilty for thinking those kinds of thoughts. My colleagues are getting laid off, left and right. Their lives are being ruined, and here I am, wishing for that! That's seriously messed up. Besides, I'd worked hard to get the job I currently had. I ought to be grateful. That's what I convinced myself to believe. I kept my head down, suppressed my feelings, and just chugged along.

Then one day, a guy named Jeff pulled me aside for a chat. Just like my boss, Jeff was an influential person at the company—a department leader, a former theater geek and actor, charismatic, funny, and beloved. Everyone sensed that Jeff was being groomed to replace the current CEO once he retired.

"Alex, we're creating a new position in my department," Jeff told me, with a warm smile. "I think you'd be a good fit. If you're interested, I encourage you to apply."

I'd always liked Jeff. And I definitely liked the sound of doing something new. He told me a little more about the new position—the responsibilities, the salary (almost double what I was currently earning), and so on. He urged me to throw my hat into the ring. So I applied.

Fairly quickly, Jeff called me in for a job interview. We had a great chat, and I felt good about my chances.

"If I get this new job in a different department..." I thought to myself, *"...maybe I'll be so much happier."*

A few weeks after that, Jeff invited me out for coffee. We walked to Caribou Coffee—which is like a Midwestern version of Starbucks with a prancing moose-like creature in the logo instead of a mermaid. We sat in the food court underneath the harsh fluorescent lights. He smiled kindly. He thanked me, again, for applying for the new position. He explained that they'd had so many qualified applicants, and that it had been a tough choice.

And then he told me, "You're not getting the job."

"Oh, that's no problem, thanks for letting me know..." is how I should have responded.

Bursting into tears is how I actually responded.

I was mortified. It was like all my emotions came bubbling up to the surface, all at once—my frustration about my career, my uncertainty about the future, my lack of purpose, and my aching desire to figure out what the hell I was supposed to be doing with my life—they were all spilling over the edge, and I literally couldn't stop myself from tearing up. I dabbed at my eyes with a Caribou Coffee napkin and willed myself to stop, stop, stop. *"Oh my god, this is so unprofessional,"* I thought to myself. *"Just stop."* But I couldn't.

Jeff was probably surprised by this reaction, but because he's a very classy guy, he barely let it show. Instead, he quietly asked,

"What's making you cry right now, Alex?"

I considered lying to Jeff and saying something like, "Oh gosh, it's just been a crazy week, please ignore all of this, please forgive me, let's just head back to the office."

Instead, I decided to tell Jeff the truth.

I told him that I was very unhappy at work. I told him that I'd applied for this new job, hoping that a more impressive job title—and a bigger paycheck—would make things feel better and reignite my passion somehow. Even though, in my heart, I knew it probably wouldn't. This was the first time I'd expressed these feelings to anyone, and it felt like such a massive relief to just... *say it.*

Jeff listened calmly, nodding, and then asked, "OK. Well, then, what's next for you?"

Instinctively, I blurted out, "I need to leave this company and do...some other type of work. I don't know what that will be, but I need to take a chance and try to figure it out."

He nodded again, and offered to help me figure out my next steps however he could. (Did I mention that Jeff is an amazing guy? He really is.)

One week later, I met with my boss and told him I'd be leaving the company. Instead of the usual "two weeks' notice," I asked for a longer transition period—a couple of months, ideally—so that I could gradually phase myself out of the department, train my replacement, and have enough time to figure out my next career move. He agreed to those terms. Just like that, it was official. I was leaving. It was happening.

Four months later, I attended a farewell party that my boss and coworkers threw for me. I hugged everyone goodbye, crumpled up the band posters decorating my cubicle, wiped off my keyboard, and walked out of that building for the last time.

Even after four months of ruminating, I still felt pretty unclear about where my career was heading next. I knew it would have something to do with "writing and words and stuff," but what exactly, I didn't know. I was taking a leap of faith—leaving my relatively safe job behind, putting myself out there as a freelance writer-ish-type of person, and hoping that things would work out OK.

In the eight years that followed—after walking away from that broadcasting job—I fought for, hustled for, created, and sometimes serendipitously received writing opportunities that I never could have even dreamed about. I collaborated with over two hundred clients on (literally) thousands of articles, websites, educational programs, books, and other materials that I got to help envision, write, edit, or produce in some capacity. I got a publishing deal. Then another. I also self-published two novels—one of which was recently optioned to be turned into a screenplay. I got my work featured on websites like *Forbes*, *HuffPost*, *Newsweek*, *Time*, *Lifehacker*, *BuzzFeed*, and other exciting places. I figured out how to make a living using my own brain, ten fingers, and a laptop. Even today, all of this is semi-unbelievable to me. But it happened. It's still happening.

Today, I've got my dream career as a full-time, self-employed writer, and the entire journey started... all because Jeff *didn't* offer me that fancy job in his department.

When Jeff told me, "Sorry, the position has gone to somebody else," that tear-soaked, heartfelt, painfully honest conversation was the catalyst that sparked *everything*.

It's bizarre when I think about how differently things could have gone. If Jeff had offered me the job, I probably would've accepted it. I might've continued working at the broadcasting company for another three, five, maybe even ten or fifteen years. Maybe I'd still be working there to this day.

The point of this story, of course, is that sometimes the situation that feels like the worst form of rejection—not getting the job, not getting the promotion, not getting the grant, client, or contract that you want—actually turns out to be a tremendous blessing.

A few years down the road, you might be kneeling on the ground in gratitude, saying to yourself: *"Thank God they didn't hire me."*

Painful as it may be, rejection can be a good thing. Rejection can force you to confront the truth about what you really want—a truth that, maybe, you haven't admitted to anyone yet, not even yourself. Once the truth is out, it can be dizzying and frightening, but also such a relief. Now, your next chapter can officially begin.

* * *

SURVIVAL TIP:

When you don't get offered a job that you applied for, remind yourself:

"Well, this is disappointing, but it's going to be OK. I am going to find—or create—some other type of job opportunity instead. One day, I might be incredibly grateful that this job didn't work out. This could be a huge blessing in disguise."

Maybe now, since you didn't get hired, you'll finally have time to write that cookbook you've been fantasizing about. Maybe now you've got time to schedule that long-overdue trip home to visit your mom and dad, and they'll finally tell you the "real story" of how they met. Maybe now you'll take a short-term job as a barista and realize that your greatest dream is to run your own coffee shop someday. Maybe now you'll call up that old colleague to catch up and, lo and behold, maybe she'll want to hire you.

There's no telling what could happen next. But whatever it is, it might be even better than any job that you tried to get in the past.

YOU'RE GOING TO SURVIVE

TAKE YOUR BROKEN HEART.

Story contributed by: Susan Hyatt.
Author. Entrepreneur. Life coach. Motivational speaker.

A Note from Alexandra:

When you're a writer, finding a literary agent is lot like
searching for a job. In many ways, it's the same process.
You have to write an enticing email about yourself—an
email that will (hopefully) capture a very busy person's
attention. You have to compile documents to prove
you've got the required experiences and skills. You have
to contact a *lot* of potential agents, cross your fingers,
and...wait. It can be a long, tedious process, and it's one
that's riddled with rejection. Most aspiring authors have
to stomach a lot of "No's" before an agent finally says, "I
think you're terrific, I love your book, and I want to help
you get a publishing deal."

My friend Susan knows all about it, because she just
went through the process herself. But her story actually
begins a decade earlier—with a shocking crime that
temporarily derailed Susan's entire life. Susan told the
entire story to me over the course of a long, emotional
phone call. (I was sobbing by the end.)

All you'll see, Susan is a true survivor, in more ways
than one. She's an inspiration for anybody who wants to
achieve a huge, daunting professional goal, and anybody
who wants to leave a positive mark on the world. Susan
took the single worst experience of her entire life—and

she transformed it into art. This is the story of how
it happened...

* * *

Susan: Ten years ago, I drove to my local pet store to
buy some dog kibble for our new puppy. It was a bright,
cheery day. The mid-afternoon light warmed my face.
I parked my SUV and walked across the lot behind the
store. I saw a man standing near the back entrance, and
I smiled politely at him as I passed by. Nothing seemed
out of the ordinary. Just another lovely day in the
suburbs of Evansville, Indiana.

The next thing I knew, I was face-down on the ground,
being dragged along the sharp gravel.

The man covered my mouth and pulled me behind a
dumpster. Then he told me that he'd kill my family if I
told anyone about this. And then—there's really no way
to make this sound "delicate" or "subtle"—he raped me.
In broad daylight. Literally two paces away from the
door of the neighborhood pet store.

If you've ever been sexually assaulted, first of all, I am
so incredibly sorry you had to endure that type of attack.
Secondly, you probably know that this type of trauma
can impact you in all kinds of complicated, unexpected,
and messy ways. Some women immediately want to tell
their family and the police. Other women want to block
out the memory and pretend it never happened because
it's just too painful to revisit. Other women blame
themselves and feel ashamed, as if the whole thing is
their fault, which it *never* is.

My response was to drive home, take a shower, and keep silent. I was traumatized and shocked, and I wasn't thinking clearly or logically. Also, I was genuinely terrified that this man would "kill my family," just as he'd promised to do. I tried to wash the attack off my body and forget all about it. I didn't tell my husband. I didn't tell a single living soul. I plastered a smile onto my face and continued onward with my life.

Then I found out I was pregnant—and I didn't know if the child was my husband's or the rapist's. I know this sounds like the plot of a twisted daytime soap opera, but it actually happened to me.

After that, I knew I had to talk to my husband and tell him about the pregnancy. In hysterical tears, I told him everything that had happened in that pet store parking lot. He held me tightly while I sobbed and spewed out all of the horrible details.

He was completely stunned. He promised me that we'd get through this. He told me that I could get therapy, counseling, anything I needed to recover from this attack, anything at all. We could try to track down this guy and press charges, if I wanted to. We could do anything I needed. He would be right by my side.

I was so grateful for my husband's unconditional support. But even with his love and encouragement, I was a complete mess. I was still reeling from the attack, and I was having frequent panic attacks and nightmares where I'd bolt awake with my heart pounding out of my chest, nauseous, dizzy, and sweating like I'd just sprinted through a marathon. I've always been a sunny, positive person, but during this chapter of my life, I didn't feel like "myself" at all. On any given day, I'd swing between feeling anxious...and feeling numb and emotionless.

Ultimately, I miscarried and lost the baby. I continued working full-time and caring for my other two kids. I went to PTA meetings and baked cookies for bake sales. I dutifully visited my therapist's office once a week. Life just sort of...carried on. But I really wasn't OK.

Even though everything about my life seemed "fine" to the casual observer, inside I was incredibly anxious, stressed, and unhappy. I couldn't figure out how to make myself feel better. My medication of choice became *food*.

I started snacking mindlessly all throughout my workday—chips, chocolate, whatever was lying around— just to distract myself from all of the complicated, uncomfortable emotions I was feeling. Back at home, after work, I'd make a huge platter of Brie cheese, bread, crackers, more chips, and wine, and I'd eat the entire thing while zoning out in front of the TV, watching shows I didn't even enjoy.

I was trying to escape my own body, trying to tune out everything I was thinking and feeling. And you know what? It worked. Food can be a really effective escape hatch, at least temporarily. But of course, eating constantly does carry some unwanted consequences.

I wound up gaining almost forty pounds in the span of just a few months. I'm a short woman with a petite build, so this felt like an enormous amount of excess weight on my frame. Now, on top of feeling distraught over the rape, and the miscarriage, I also felt ashamed for not having enough willpower to eat properly and stay thin. Misery on top of misery.

For about a year, I tried every diet known to womankind. Weight Watchers. South Beach. Atkins. Jenny Craig. I counted calories, carbs, and points. I boiled vats of tasteless, bland, low-sodium cabbage soup. I starved myself with carrot sticks, celery stalks, and sugar-free candies, and then binged on massive plates of enchiladas to "reward" myself for being so "good."

I got myself into a sick, twisted cycle of dieting and bingeing, losing and regaining, over and over and over. At one point, my body was so malnourished and depleted from the constant dieting, my hair started to fall out.

Watching those blonde strands swirl down the shower drain, I had an epiphany.

"This shouldn't be happening. I need to stop dieting and figure out some other way to lose weight, because this isn't healthy."

It didn't happen overnight, but in the months that followed, I figured out how to start treating my body like a friend instead of an enemy.

I taught myself how to slow down and actually taste and savor my food, instead of stuffing myself mindlessly. I decluttered my closet and got rid of my "beige, boring mom" clothes—anything that made me feel tired or frumpy. I decluttered my circle of friends, too, and I ended a couple of relationships. Back then, I had a lot of "friends" who didn't act like true friends at all, and who only wanted to get together to eat poorly, drink, and complain about their bodies, whine about their husbands, or gossip about other women. I didn't want that type of negativity rubbing off on me anymore, so I distanced myself from those people. It was like a "detox" for my social life. I felt lighter and happier immediately.

I also challenged myself to be a little braver, and to do things that scared me. Little things, like posing for a family photo with my kids, even though I didn't feel "thin enough" yet. Gradually, I challenged myself to do bigger things, like enrolling in a certification program to become a life coach, and eventually, quitting my job in real estate so that I could do coaching full-time.

Week by week, month by month, I continued to shed all types of things: old clothes that I didn't like wearing, depressing diet books, stacks of magazines filled with unrealistic images, toxic relationships, and social obligations that bored me.

As I continued to strip away everything that had been weighing me down, an amazing thing happened: I lost weight, too. It happened gradually and naturally, without any calorie-counting or obsessive behavior. It just... happened.

My entire life was transforming, and my body was transforming right along with it.

It felt like a miracle—and it was a miracle that I wanted to share with as many women as possible.

In the years that followed, I started offering weight loss coaching to women in my community, and then eventually to clients that I met online, based all over the world. Women loved hearing my personal story of transformation, and they loved my *"no diet"* approach to weight loss, which felt so different from anything they'd been encouraged to do before. Over and over, clients emailed me to say "I'm losing weight, just like you said I would, but that's just the beginning. I also found the courage to apply for my dream job!" or "I finally launched my online jewelry shop!" or "I booked that vacation that I've been putting off forever!" or "I asked that cute guy at the dog park out on a date."

I noticed a distinct pattern: when women stop dieting, and stop obsessing over their size, ironically, *that's* when they finally start losing weight. In the process, they become braver and bolder. They start asking for raises at work. They start demanding more help around the house. They lunge after exciting opportunities instead of hiding and waiting until "later." Their lives expand in all kinds of ways. This isn't just about "weight loss." It's a female empowerment revolution. It's about treating yourself like a woman who matters, and who's worthy of respect.

I wanted to write a book about my story—a book that would guide women through a weight loss process unlike anything they'd seen or tried before. My clients told me, "Yes! I'd buy that book in a heartbeat." My Facebook community—which had grown to over ten thousand fans by this point—echoed the excitement. "Do it!" "Write it!"

"I want to buy a copy for my daughter!" "Please write it ASAP."

I holed up for five days with Alexandra, my writing mentor, and poured out the book. Hundreds and hundreds of pages of material. Stories from my own life. Stories from my clients' lives. Specific, actionable guidance on how to lose weight without harming yourself in the process—and guidance on how to become braver and feel unstoppable.

After that, we created a very detailed book proposal to describe why this book needed to get published, and why it would be a smash-hit success and sell millions of copies. (Well, hopefully!)

With that, it was time for me to start emailing literary agents. I needed to find someone who would believe in this book as much as I did.

I wish I could say that it was a quick and easy process. I wish I could tell you that I woke up the very next morning and three agents had already emailed me to say, "I love you! Your book is a work of sheer genius!"

But, no. That's not what happened. What actually happened is...I contacted twelve different agents. And I received twelve rejections. Bam, bam, bam. One after another.

A few agents were actually pretty rude to me, and basically told me:

"Customers want diet books, and this isn't a diet book, so I don't think any publisher will be interested in this project."

I wanted to email back with a sassy tone and say:

"Yeah, I *know* it's not a diet book. Because diets *suck* and they *ruin* women's lives. That's literally the entire point of my book."

(I restrained myself from saying that, but just barely.)

After receiving the twelfth rejection in a row, I started to cry. Hot, sloppy, messy tears, while clutching my iPhone in my car outside the gym. I'm a strong woman, but twelve "No's" is a lot for anybody to stomach.

I felt so misunderstood. Why couldn't anyone "see" what I was trying to achieve with this book? Why didn't they understand that I was trying to save women's lives, crush the diet industry, and start a health revolution? Why wasn't that message coming across clearly? What was I "missing" here?

I have to admit: I felt really defeated and irritated. For a while, I stopped emailing agents. I just completely stopped trying. For about six months, I put my book on the backburner and busied myself with other projects, like working with clients, leading retreats, and doing speaking engagements. It was a full, exciting, and very profitable year for my coaching practice, and there were plenty of other projects to distract me from the book. But oh...the book. The book kept nagging at me the entire time, saying, *"Please don't forget about me."*

My clients kept nagging me, too. "Did you find an agent yet?" "Whatever happened with your book?" "When is the book coming out?" "When can I pre-order it?"

The end of the year was fast approaching. I stared at my calendar. I stared at the book proposal Word document that had been sitting on my computer desktop for ages, ignored and unattended. And I realized: *"I can't procrastinate anymore. It's time to find a literary agent, get a book deal, and get this book into bookstores. I've got to try again."*

I freshened up my book proposal, made a new list of agents to contact, and dove back into the boiling water, headfirst.

Then I had...a gutsy idea.

There was one literary agent that I had contacted many months ago. She'd said "No thanks" to my book concept, but unlike some of the other agents, she had been very kind and gracious about it. My intuition told me to circle back and pitch her again. So I did.

I told her, "I've revamped my book proposal. It's better than ever. I've attached it to this email, just in case you'd like to review it again." At the bottom of my email, I included a link to a video clip of Beyoncé strutting into a room in queenly attire, wearing a crown, to let her know, "I mean business." She loved that.

"Anybody who includes a Beyoncé clip in their email is someone I want to know," she told me. She reviewed my sparkly new proposal—and she was impressed. She wanted to talk on the phone ASAP. Less than two weeks later, the ink was dry on the contract, and I officially had a big-shot literary agent. Lifelong goal: *achieved.*

I know that I'm going to see my book on bookshelves someday soon. I have the manuscript, I have the agent, I have deep determination, and it's all just a matter of time. It's been a long, winding road to get to this point in my career, filled with so much heartache. As Oprah might say, here's what I know for sure:

1. You've got to "take your broken heart and turn it into art."

That's a direct quote from the late, great actress Carrie Fisher. The absolute worst thing that's ever happened to you? Most likely, that's a goldmine of material for you to write about, speak about, and sing about. People want to hear the story of how you survived. We all need, crave, yearn for those types of stories. You story will make other people stronger when they hear it.

2. Just because someone says "No" once doesn't mean it's a "No" forever.

I circled back to an agent who had rejected me in the past. The second time around, she said "Yes." Don't be afraid to swing back to a company, client, or agent who wasn't interested in you before. Things might be different now. *You* might be different now.

3. If there's a project or goal that's burning in your heart, begging to be completed, don't ignore it.

Don't leave it on the backburner forever. You'll regret it.

And lastly, to whomever is reading this story, remember that the founder of Pandora received three hundred rejections before getting funding for his project. J.K. Rowling received twelve "No's" before a publisher expressed interest in *Harry Potter*. Mark Ruffalo went on six hundred auditions before landing his first acting role.

Take courage from those people's stories—and from mine. Dust off your shoulders and put yourself back into the ring. You've got to be tenacious, courageous, and willing to tolerate the temporary moments of discouragement that will inevitably arise.

Get back in there. One more letter. One more revision. One more try.

Your big break could be one email away.

* * *

SURVIVAL TIP:

Don't be afraid to contact someone more than once. The start-up company that couldn't afford to hire you last year might be in a totally different position today. Maybe now they've got plenty of funding and they'd love to hire someone like you. The literary agent who said

"No" to your initial proposal might be impressed by your second revision. "No thanks" is not always a permanent decision. Be gutsy, be persistent, and try again.

Also: *"Take your broken heart and turn it into art."*

The worst experience of your life can become the spark, the fuel, the inspiration for the greatest thing you ever make.

I'VE ALREADY WON.

Story contributed by: Niki Driscoll.
Author. Athlete. Nutrition and food cravings consultant.

A Note from Alexandra:

As a kid, I was painfully shy and unathletic. I hated sports. I loathed PE class. I was terrified of getting smacked in the face with a basketball. I couldn't swing a softball bat to save my life. Running sent me into fits of asthmatic wheezing.

One time, on a school field trip, a classmate dared me to climb up a swinging ladder thingy. It was a high-stakes dare. If I chickened out or couldn't make it to the top, then I had to eat ashes. Like, actual ashes from a campfire. (Why there was a blazing campfire, a tall ladder, and apparently no adult supervision, I cannot recall! Well, I guess it's because it was the early nineties—the pre-smartphone era, before parents tracked their kids' movements with GPS systems.)

Obviously, I couldn't climb the swinging ladder thingy. So of course, I had to eat ashes. While everybody watched.

I was horrified. I kinda thought if I ate ashes, you know, maybe I'd...die? So I tried to cheat by eating a tiny speck of blackened marshmallow dust instead of real ashes, but oh, my classmate was wise to that game! He called me out—*"That's not real ash! Faker! Faker!"*—in front of the other kids, who stared at me with disgusted expressions.

After all, there's only one thing worse than a non-athletic, asthmatic nerdball—and that's a non-athletic, asthmatic nerdball who's also a *cheater* and a *faker*.

Fortunately, shortly after that incident, someone found the word "penis" in the dictionary and then everyone was distracted by that revelation and forgot all about me.

Suffice it to say: when it came to athletics, I was a dud. The kid you picked last. The kid you didn't want on your team because she was a liability, not a helpful addition.

By age eight or nine, I had accepted the reality of my situation: I was a useless blob. I usually found some way of avoiding PE class—excuses, feigned illness, actual illness, bribery, persuasive rhetoric. Reading in the library made me happy. Sports did not.

Then one day, a teacher encouraged my parents to sign me up for dance classes. It would be a good way for me to get some exercise, she thought. Maybe I'd enjoy dancing more than regular sports. And maybe dancing would improve my posture, make me a little less clumsy, and transform me into a beautiful, confident, graceful butterfly. Et cetera.

My parents found an after-school dance program and signed me up. Much to their surprise, and mine, I immediately loved it.

Now, let's be clear, I wasn't the greatest dancer in the entire world. Even after seven years of dance classes, I still wasn't Martha Graham or Mikhail Baryshnikov. But I truly loved it.

Dancing felt like "acting," in a way. When I was dancing, I could temporarily pretend to be someone else—a village maiden, a handsome prince, a sugarplum queen, a cursed girl cruelly trapped in a swan's body. I could express the kinds of feelings that I couldn't put into words. I loved training. I loved rehearsing. I loved performing. What I didn't love was...auditioning.

Three or four times a year, my dance school would put together a big performance. Sometimes it was a full-length ballet. Sometimes it was a variety show with tap dancing, jazz, hip hop, and so forth. Each time, you had to audition in front of the teachers.

First, they'd watch you dance for a few minutes with blank, expressionless faces. Then you had to line up with all the other dancers, in order of height, facing yourself in the mirror. The teachers would pace back and forth, staring back at you, scanning you up and down, quietly murmuring things to one another, and making notes on a clipboard.

Then a few days later, they'd post a list in the hallway of the dance studio. You'd scurry up and search for your name. And that's how you'd find out if you got a fantastic part in the show—like Queen of the Flowers—or a less-desirable part—like Background Rat Number Seven.

I absolutely *hated* the audition process. To me, it always felt awkward and stressful, and it twisted my stomach into knots. It was kind of like a job interview—except instead of having a private conversation in an air-conditioned office with one hiring manager, you're having your "interview" in a brightly lit mirrored studio, wearing a tiny leotard, standing shoulder-to-shoulder with forty other people who all want the same job as you.

Yikes.

I've always had the utmost respect for professional dancers, actors, and athletes—people who have to do auditions and tryouts over and over and over. Sometimes, multiple times a week, or even multiple times a day. I've always wondered, *"Good Lord. How do they do that?"* It must feel stressful and exhausting every single time...right?

As I learned from the next storyteller, Niki Driscoll... that's not necessarily the case.

As she explained to me, auditioning doesn't have to be an exhausting, demoralizing process. Auditioning can actually be really exciting, empowering, and fun—even if you don't get selected. You can leave any audition—or job interview—feeling proud of yourself. You can walk away feeling like, *"I've already won."* Even if you don't get hired.

How on earth is that possible? Well, I'll let her tell you...

* * *

Niki: My mother badgered me into joining the pep squad in the fifth grade.

This wasn't a high-pressure situation. There were no tryouts. Anyone who wanted to participate was welcome to join the squad. Even so, I was paralyzed with anxiety.

I was afraid of looking stupid, being perceived as ugly, messing up a dance routine, and being whispered about behind my back. During each pep rally, my movements were timid and I only mouthed the words—no sound actually emerged. Peppy? Not exactly. Yet—despite my timidity—a big part of me loved performing in front of an audience. I had caught the "cheerleader fever." I yearned for a chance to do it again.

Years later, I tried out for the cheerleading squad at my high school. I didn't get selected. I tried to make the squad multiple times. No success. I'd replay the tryouts in my mind, over and over, tormented with humiliation.

Eventually, I stopped trying to be a cheerleader. I joined the running team instead. Turns out, I was good at it. With cross-country running, I could shed my insecurities. Each competition literally allowed me to disappear into the woods.

While I excelled at running, the yearning to dance, cheer, and perform never left me. Some people are just born to cheer! At various points in my life, complete strangers have asked me, "Are you a cheerleader?" The question always created a regret-filled lump in my throat because in high school and college, I was never given the chance.

My desire to perform did not dissipate with age—it only grew stronger. Except there aren't a ton of opportunities for a thirty-year-old woman with a full-time job and two kids to twirl onto a football field and shake her pom-poms in the air.

Maybe the opportunity was long gone.

Maybe I'd never get to realize my dream.

Maybe...

But some part of me just couldn't accept that.

At age thirty, I decided to train for a bikini competition, a type of bodybuilding where you are judged based on your physique, particularly muscle symmetry, as well as your stage presence and personality. In some ways, it's like cheerleading, but without the leaping and cartwheels.

After months of training and preparation, the big competition arrived. I stepped onstage, baking under the bright spotlights. The music played. I struck my first pose. I vowed to stay centered, channeling positivity and enthusiasm.

It wasn't easy. The judges were...very judge-y. They all wore looks on their faces that made you feel like a product of obvious self-delusion—like you didn't belong there. I tuned them out and kept telling myself to embody the energy of the feminine, the divine, and pure joy. Silently, inside my mind, as I moved from pose to pose, I repeated over and over to myself, *"I am feminine. Divine. Pure joy."*

And you know what? I rocked my first competition, placing in the top five against women a decade younger than me. It gave me a surge of confidence. I promised myself that I would keep pursuing opportunities to perform.

I kept that promise.

A few years after my first bikini competition, a friend and former NFL team member suggested that I try out for the Saintsations—the official cheerleading squad for the New Orleans Saints.

It was just two weeks before tryouts. I had already missed both preparatory workshops, and the rest of the contestants had been practicing for six weeks. It was a total long shot because I was woefully under-prepared. But I wanted to put myself out there anyway—to test my emotional control.

Would I be able to maintain a smile on my face, enjoy performing, and genuinely have fun—even if I felt completely out of my league? It was sure to be an interesting challenge.

My rules were simple:

1. No comparing myself with the other women.

2. If I forgot a portion of the choreography, I had to maintain my confident, upbeat energy and move on immediately without pausing.

3. No self-berating. I will be kind to myself.

I followed those rules—and my Saintsations audition was one of the best performances of my life. I messed up a couple of times, but I maintained my poise and had a ridiculous amount of fun.

In the end, I was not chosen to join the Saintsations, but I did make it through the first round of cuts, and I was the happiest girl on the planet—floating on air, so proud of myself. I brought joy and excitement into the audition and it showed.

I've learned that when I'm facing a critical panel of judges, the best thing to do is to ignore their stern facial expressions and to focus on the persona I want to project into the room. By repeating a phrase like *"I am feminine. Divine. Pure joy."* inside of my mind, I can step into that role and express those qualities with every cell in my body. It's like "acting," except the difference is that I've trained myself to believe it's true.

I've also learned that it is very powerful to set your own personal rules for competitions or any other situation where you're being judged or critiqued. This feels so amazing, because it puts the power back in your hands. Rather than relying on the judges' decision to feel validated, you can validate yourself.

If your rules are...

1. I'm here to have fun.

2. I'm not going to berate myself.

3. I'm going to fill the room with positive energy.

...and you succeed in following those rules, then you've already won.

* * *

SURVIVAL TIP:

If you've got an audition, a job interview, an important meeting, or a networking event coming up soon, create some "personal rules" that you intend to follow. If you don't like the word "rule," you can call these "guidelines" or "policies" or "intentions."

You might decide:

1. I will ask three people, "What was the best part of your day so far?"

2. I will to introduce Sharon to Nicholas, because I have a feeling they'd hit it off.

3. I will find someone who looks bored and lonely and I'll chat with them.

4. I will not compare myself to anybody else.

5. I will brighten the room and spread positivity.

If you succeed in following your own personal rules, then you can leave that interview, audition, meeting, or event feeling proud of yourself. Regardless of what happens next, you'll know that you did what you intended to do.

How Hard are You Trying, Really?

My friend Susan (remember her story from a few pages ago?) has a teenage daughter named Emily. Emily is one of those teenagers who seems much older and wiser than any sixteen-year-old could possibly be. She's funny.

She's thoughtful. She knows far more about history and politics than most grown-ups. When (when, not "if") Emily runs for President, she's got my vote.

During her sophomore year in high school, Emily started her own theater company. But not just any theater company. It's a revolutionary theater company that produces classic plays and Broadway musicals—but with an all-female cast. *The Tempest*—with a female Prospero. *Les Misérables*—with a female Javert. *1776*—with a female Ben Franklin. You get the idea.

Emily wants to give women and girls the chance to play all of the amazing, exciting roles that are typically reserved for men and boys. She wants to make a statement about women's roles in our society: *"We're not hiding in the back row anymore. We're not playing the 'less-important' parts anymore. We want full access to all of the same opportunities as men. We want to be center-stage."*

Did I mention she's sixteen years old?

#EmilyForPresident

Shortly after launching her theater company, Emily found herself facing a problem: she couldn't find enough women who wanted to audition to be in her first show. She needed twenty-two cast members, but so far, she only had ten.

The first rehearsal session was fast approaching. Emily started to panic. Even though she's an incredibly courageous young woman, this particular obstacle felt like...too much to handle.

With tears in her eyes, Emily told her mom, Susan, "I can't see how I'm going to find twelve more cast members in the next couple weeks. I don't know what to do. I've already asked *everybody*."

Emily felt completely discouraged. Like maybe this whole theater company was going to fail before the very first rehearsal even happened. Like maybe the whole thing was a dumb idea.

Her mom listened and then said, "OK, Em. You said you've asked 'everybody'. Who is 'everybody'? How many people have you asked to audition exactly?"

Emily thought about it, and then said, "Fifteen people."

Susan said, "OK. We live in a city with over one hundred thousand people. Fifteen people is just a tiny fraction of our population. 'Fifteen people' is not 'everybody.' Not even remotely close. If you want to find twelve more cast members, you need to contact a lot more than just fifteen people."

I'm happy to report: Emily listened to her smart mom. She pulled herself together and—with her mom's help—she came up with a fresh strategy to find twelve more cast members. They started texting, emailing, calling, putting up new flyers all around town, and pounding the pavement. Their efforts paid off. Within twenty-four hours, Emily found four more cast members. Boomshaka-laka! Success! Their efforts paid off, and the project was back on track.

Emily's predicament feels so relatable to me. Maybe for you, too?

So often in life, when we're facing a challenge, we say to ourselves: "Ugh! This is impossible! I've contacted everybody! I've tried everything!"

But...really?

Everybody?

Everything?

You sure about that?

When we take a step back and look at the numbers, we typically discover that we haven't actually talked to "everybody" and we haven't tried "everything." Not even close.

OK, sure. Maybe you talked to ten people about your project. "Ten people" is not "everybody." Maybe you applied for five scholarships. Five scholarships is not "every scholarship." Maybe you told seven people that you're searching for a new job. Seven people is not "everybody." Seven people is just...seven people. There are seven billion people on planet earth. Seven people is a microscopic fraction of the human population.

Your mind is tricking you, trying to convince you that you've made such a huge effort when in reality...maybe that's not actually true.

I fell into this mental trap a few years ago. It was right before my first book was scheduled to hit the shelves. I wanted to promote the book, and I got this notion that I should be on TV. I came up with a fun idea for a morning talk show segment.

I emailed a producer at the local TV news station to pitch my idea. I didn't hear back, so I emailed again. No response. Then I pulled out the big guns. I recorded a voice note—a little MP3 file explaining my TV segment idea—and I attached that MP3 to my third email.

"Oh yeah!" I thought to myself. *"Nobody sends a voice note. That's really going to make my email stand out. They'll definitely contact me after hearing this."*

Nope. No response.

After that, I felt so dejected and confused.

"But...but...I emailed three times! And I even recorded a voice note!"

And yet, they still didn't invite me to appear on TV. It made no sense to me. In my mind, I had tried "everything."

Looking back, I have to laugh at myself, because obviously...I didn't try "everything." I sent a couple of emails. Sure, I made an effort to get myself booked on TV, but all things considered, I made a relatively small effort. I didn't do "everything." I did "a couple things." I could have made a much bigger effort to achieve my goal.

For starters, I could have put together an impressive media packet. I could have mailed that packet to the TV station. Or I could have dropped it off in person. I could have asked all of my friends for help. *"Do you know anyone who works in TV? Could you make an introduction for me?"* I could have attended events where journalists and TV producers hang out. I could have marched up and introduced myself. But I didn't do any of those things, because I was too lazy and timid. Instead, I hid in my apartment, fired off a couple quick emails, and called it a day. And then I whined when I didn't get what I wanted. That's the unpleasant truth.

We all slip into this kind of thinking. We all get frustrated, tired, and discouraged. It's happened to me, many times. It happened to Emily. It's probably happened to you, too.

Maybe you say you're "so ready" for an exciting new job, promotion, or some other big career opportunity, but then instead of making a full-hearted effort to get what you want, you made a half-hearted effort. Or a quarter-hearted effort.

The truth is, most of the time, we're not operating at full capacity. Not even close. We refuse to dig deep. We make excuses. We flake out. We hold back. We send off one or two emails and then we grumble when we don't get what we want. As Emily's wise mom once said to me, it's fine if you want to hold back. It's fine if you want to Netflix and Chill. But if that's what you choose, well, then...

"Don't be mad about the results you didn't get from the work you didn't do."

I'm not advocating that anybody push themselves to the point of injury, burnout, or adrenal failure. I'm all for balance and relaxation. I literally have three beds in my one-bedroom apartment: sleeping bed, TV-watching-and-sometimes-guest bed, and outside-balcony bed.

What I'm saying—mostly to myself, because I need to re-relearn this lesson continually—is that before you decide that your dream is "impossible" or that it's "taking too long to find a new job," check in with yourself. Do an honest assessment of your efforts. See if you're actually trying as hard as you could be.

And if you haven't been trying that hard, hey, that's OK. That doesn't make you a bad person. It just makes you a person who's facing some important choices:

Give up—or go harder?

Accept defeat—or try again?

Hide in your bedroom behind your laptop screen—or get outside, talk to actual people, and be gutsy and brave?

Convince yourself you've tried everything—or *actually* try? This time, with feeling?

What's it going to be?

* * *

SURVIVAL TIP:

The next time you feel discouraged because you feel like you've "tried everything," take a cue from Emily and Emily's mom, and make a list of what you've *actually* done.

How many people have you *actually* contacted? How many jobs have you *actually* applied for? How many events have you *actually* attended? How many informational interviews have you lined up? How many of your friends, family members, colleagues, and classmates have you contacted to ask for help? And so on.

Make a list. Look at the numbers. Have you truly pursued every possible opportunity? Have you been making a full-hearted effort, or a half-hearted effort?

When we tell ourselves, *"Ugh. I've already tried everything,"* we're usually being delusional. Most likely, you haven't tried everything. Most likely, you've just barely scratched the surface.

Try again. This time, with your whole heart. This time, put some muscle into it.

Watch what happens next.

THE UNIVERSE HAD BETTER PLANS FOR ME.

Story contributed by: Robert Hartwell.
Actor. Singer. Dancer. Choreographer. Founder of The
Broadway Dance Collective.

A Note from Alexandra:

It was late afternoon. I was settling into my chair on the
sixth floor of an opulent NYC hotel. I'd been invited to
attend an ultra-fancy high tea party. But not just any
tea party. It was a client's ten-year business anniversary
party, and the room was filled with fascinating
entrepreneurs, consultants, literary agents, and other
creative types. The atmosphere was elegant and refined,
like a scene straight out of *Downton Abbey*. Porcelain
tea pots. Tiny sandwiches. Currant scones and cream.
Champagne and chocolate-dipped strawberries. The
whole nine yards. I kept smoothing out my hair, hoping I
looked relatively presentable.

"Everyone, everyone, this is Robert, and he has a
surprise for us," my client announced, tinkling her spoon
onto her champagne glass to get our attention.

Robert rose from his chair—impeccably dressed in an
electric blue suit with a pink and purple cravat—marched
over to the speakers, flipped a switch, and suddenly the
room was filled with...Beyoncé.

"Ladies, we're going to get a little nasty. You OK with
that?" Robert asked.

Oh yes. We were OK with that.

Robert explained that—before sipping our tea—we were all going to learn a synchronized dance number. A few women in the room looked slightly horrified. *"Dancing? Here? Now?"* But Robert launched into the sequence, and within minutes, he had every single woman in the room swiveling, shimmying, snapping, and stomping around. The dance culminated with a booty-popping moment and a dramatic hair flip. Everyone participated. No one refused. Robert's energy was completely infectious, and we all got swept up in the delightful madness of it all. (The hotel staff enjoyed a pretty unforgettable show, too!)

Needless to say, it was the best tea party I've ever attended. Towards the end of the event, I gave Robert a massive hug, we exchanged phone numbers, and I knew we were going to become instantaneous friends. I also had a feeling that I ought to interview him for this book. *"I bet he's got a story or two,"* I thought to myself. And he certainly does.

As a long-time Broadway performer, Robert's career is riddled with Survival Stories. He has endured all kinds of rejection and discouragement, not to mention blatant racism. He told the following story to me over the phone, and at the end, all I could say was…"Whoa."

For anyone who has ever wondered, *"Why didn't they choose me? Why didn't I get the job? I worked so hard, and I know I was the right person for the gig. . ."* Robert's story is dedicated to you.

* * *

Robert: I was working on my third Broadway show—
Rodgers and Hammerstein's *Cinderella*—and I'd been
cast in the ensemble. It was a fabulous, magical, surreal
experience. It felt like my very own "fairy tale," in a way.
After so many years of hard work and training, finally,
I'd made it. I was part of a hit Broadway show, and I was
living my dream life.

In that particular production, I was the only black
person in the ensemble cast. Knowing this, I felt a lot of
pressure to be absolutely flawless and never miss a single
show. I almost never took days off, because if I did, that
would mean...there would be no diversity in Cinderella's
magical kingdom! I thought about the non-white kids
sitting in the audience, and I felt a huge responsibility to
them to show up every single night. And I did.

After performing in *Cinderella* for quite a while, an
unexpected opportunity came into my life. A super-
famous Broadway director came to see the show, saw
me perform, and then asked me to be part of a brand
new project that she was developing. This woman was
like a *god* to me. She's a living legend, she's won tons of
Tony Awards, and she's hugely respected in the theater
world. And she wanted *me* to be part of her new show? I
almost died.

Creating a new Broadway show doesn't happen
overnight. It's a gradual process with many, many
phases. First, there's the pre-production phase. That's
where the director gathers together some temporary

cast members and starts to piece the show together. She asked me to be part of the pre-production process. I enthusiastically agreed. Of course! I was thrilled!

I started doing double-duty. Every morning, I'd go to pre-production rehearsals from 9:00 a.m. to 4:00 p.m., then I'd have a quick break, then I'd report to the theater for my "other" job performing in *Cinderella*. I had pre-production five to six days a week, and then *Cinderella* performances eight times a week. It was a brutal schedule. I pushed my body to the absolute limit. But I wanted to impress this legendary director, so even though I felt exhausted nearly all the time, I *never* let it show. I always showed up early and I made sure she could see how reliable I was. I felt so proud to be working with her, and I just wanted to make a stellar impression.

After the pre-production stage comes the reading. That's where you put on a performance—not a full-out performance with full costumes and lighting and everything, but more like a stripped-down, bare-bones performance, just so that the show's team and potential investors can get a sense of what it's all about.

The reading went so well. Amazingly well. This new show was brilliantly funny. Everyone was laughing and the room was buzzing with excitement. I remember thinking to myself, *"I think this show is going to be a huge hit."*

Finally, after pre-production and the reading, it was time for the auditions. In other words, it was time for the directors and producers to choose the cast members who would appear on Broadway in the real, actual show.

This was the moment I'd been waiting for. I loved being in *Cinderella,* but I was ready for a new challenge and was completely emotionally invested in this new show. I couldn't wait to audition and officially get my spot.

The first audition went great. I made the cut and got called back for another audition. That went great, too. I got another call-back. Then another. And then it was time for the final auditions.

The night before the final auditions, I was hanging out in my dressing room backstage at *Cinderella.* I shared the room with my castmate and best friend, Andy. He's a tall, blonde-haired guy with a classic, "American hunk" look, plus he's incredibly kind and talented. We'd both been auditioning for the new show, and we'd both made it to the final auditions. It was so exciting. A few minutes before the curtain went up, Andy checked his phone and said, "Oh, awesome! I just got a text. My final audition appointment is going to be 9:00 a.m. tomorrow. What time is yours?"

I grabbed my phone to see if I'd gotten a text, too. But I hadn't.

"Oh, I'm not sure," I said to Andy. I felt a sick, awful feeling in the pit of my stomach, but I tried to brush it aside. "I'm sure they'll text me any moment," I told myself. Meanwhile, we had a show to do. We went onstage and did the first act of *Cinderella.* At intermission, I dashed back to my dressing room and checked my phone again. Still no text. Feeling sickened, I called my agent. He answered and said, "Oh Robert,

I'm so sorry, but they've decided not to move forward with you."

To say that I was "devastated" is putting it mildly. I was stunned. Shell-shocked. I literally could not believe it. I had worked like a maniac all throughout the pre-production, the reading, and the numerous auditions. I'd sung, acted, and danced my ass off. I'd gotten up at the crack of dawn and hauled across town so I could be on time every single day. I'd gotten positive, glowing feedback all the way through. And now, at the very last moment, after all of that...I'm not getting the job? But why?

Andy popped back into the dressing room to get ready for act two. I must have looked nauseous, and he immediately knew something was wrong. He came over and pulled me into a hug. I broke down and started sobbing. Somehow, I pulled myself together and finished that night's performance of *Cinderella*. Then I went home to my apartment, called my mom, and cried until I fell asleep.

The next day, I woke up and felt slightly crazed. I couldn't accept that I hadn't been chosen. I needed answers. Privately, I started texting and calling some of my colleagues—assistant directors, associate producers, people who might be able to explain why I hadn't been cast in the new show. I'd never done anything like this before, but for whatever reason, I felt like I couldn't rest until I had answers.

Finally, I got ahold of someone who told me the truth. He said, "Robert, you are so terrific, and everyone loved working with you. But," he continued, in a whispered tone, "just between you and me, the directors were not looking to have any black people in the show. The show is set in the 1920s, in a particular era, in a particular setting and economic class, and they wanted the show to look historically accurate."

Historically accurate? So in other words...white. Hearing this, my worst fears were confirmed. I felt wounded, overlooked, unappreciated, betrayed...every emotion imaginable.

Meanwhile, my best friend Andy booked the job and got cast as the understudy to the leading role—which was a huge professional victory for him. I was so happy for Andy. He's an incredible human being, and he absolutely deserved to book the role. But it was a really difficult time for me. For several weeks, I felt so angry—not towards my friend Andy, but towards the entire situation. Eventually, I realized that I needed to let it go. I couldn't keep walking around carrying all of this heavy anger inside of me. It was making me feel sick. And then before too long—as often happens in the theater world—another unexpected opportunity came up. My agent called to tell me about a new production of *Motown: The Musical*, which was departing soon for a nationwide tour.

"Do you want to audition?" he asked, and I said, "Absolutely. *Yes*."

I auditioned and got in. Just like that, I got offered a one-year contract with a great salary. This meant financial security, along with a chance to travel across America and see the entire country. I'd be able to save money and make the rest of my student loan payments. Plus, *Motown* had simpler choreography that wasn't quite as hard on my body, which meant I'd be able to perform nightly without completely burning myself to the ground. At that time, I felt incredibly tired, physically and emotionally, and I needed a break from NYC, so the *Motown* opportunity felt perfect on so many levels. I signed the one-year contract and I knew in my heart: *"This is the right move for me."*

A few days before I left town to start the *Motown* adventure, I was clicking around, reading a few theater news websites and blogs, and I noticed a shocking announcement. The glitzy 1920s show—the one that hadn't cast me—was closing after just a few months on Broadway. The investors had poured millions into the production, but tickets weren't selling, the critical reviews had been mediocre, and audiences didn't seem impressed. The show was a flop. I was stunned, and I thought to myself, *"If I'd gotten cast in that show like I wanted, then I'd be out of a job right now."*

In that moment, I felt as though God, or the Universe, whatever term you want to use, had been looking out for me the entire time. I'd been so obsessed with getting cast in one particular show, and when it didn't happen, I was devastated. But meanwhile...the Universe was like, "Just be patient, Robert. We've got a much, much better plan for you. Just you wait and see."

The Universe was right about that. The *Motown* tour ended up being one of the peak experiences of my entire life. I ended up touring with that show for three years. I visited almost every city in the country. I saw cornfields and mountains and skyscrapers. I met an amazing guy in the cast and had my first real, deep relationship, which was so beautiful. So many incredible things happened for me on that tour, and to think...the only reason it happened is because I got rejected from a different job first.

What I've learned is that when you think the Universe is being so cruel and unfair to you, maybe that's not actually true. Maybe the Universe is taking good care of you, or even protecting you from disaster, or setting you up for another opportunity that's one million times better, and you just don't know it yet. But soon? You'll see.

* * *

SURVIVAL TIP:

When you go after a job that you really want—and you don't get it—it can feel totally crushing. You might think to yourself: "This is the *only* job in the entire *world* that's perfect for me! I missed my chance. Now everything's ruined. I'll never get another opportunity like this again." But that's just not true.

There are over twenty-seven million businesses in the United States, millions more across the world, and an infinite number of ways that you could start your own business, too. There are over twenty-five thousand universities in the world that you could work for or study at. There are thousands of theaters and performing arts centers. There are so many companies you could work for, so many projects you could be involved in, so many exciting possibilities. If one job doesn't work out, you've (literally) got millions of other options.

Plus, as Robert's story illustrates, the job you desperately want might *not* be a good move for you. It could wind up being deeply disappointing or even disastrous! Later on, you might feel grateful it didn't work out. So, shake off the disappointment and move on. Instead of staring into the past, focus on your next opportunity and your next move. There's no scarcity. Remind yourself: *"I've got plenty of options."*

Every Door Can Be Unlocked.

Shortly after quitting my job at the public broadcasting company, I happened to meet a woman named Megan, the director of a local branding and marketing agency. It was a snazzy, fancy agency with lots of big-name clients—major universities, hospitals, and banks—and they'd won numerous awards for their work. I mentioned that I had recently left my previous position, and that now I was a freelance writer. Megan said, "Well, we're always looking for good copywriters," and invited me out for coffee.

I was ecstatic and slightly star-struck. I barely knew this woman, but I could tell she was smart, stylish, cool, and seriously successful. Of course, I wanted to impress her.

At our coffee date, I told her about my experiences as a student journalist in college, and my work at the broadcasting company. I showed her my (admittedly, very small) portfolio of articles, interviews, and other pieces of writing that I'd done in the past.

She listened intently and was very kind and supportive. She congratulated me on quitting my nine-to-five job and diving into the uncertain waters of freelancing.

"It takes a lot of courage to be self-employed," she told me. "I like your spirit."

"But...?" I wondered. Something in her tone told me that a *"But"* was about to drop like a sledgehammer.

"But you don't seem to have any copywriting experience. I'm sorry, but I can't hire you unless I can see some copywriting work in your portfolio."

She encouraged me to stay in touch, and to email her again in a year or two, after I'd accumulated some copywriting samples that I could show her.

We shook hands and parted ways.

I felt completely deflated—like a total rookie, a loser, a nobody. I really wanted to get a copywriting gig, but to do that, I needed to provide samples of my previous copywriting work. But how was I supposed to get samples of copywriting work unless somebody hired me for a copywriting job first? It felt like a Catch-22.

Back at home, I plopped myself in front of my laptop and considered my options. I could send Megan a polite email to say, "Thanks for meeting with me today," and just leave it at that. Or...not. Maybe there was something else I could do to catch her attention and persuade her to give me a chance. Hmm. Maybe. But what?

I replayed our conversation in my mind, and I remembered something intriguing.

In the middle of our coffee date, Megan had mentioned— very briefly—that she was in the midst of rebranding her agency. They were working on a new website, rolling out some new services, and freshening up the company on many levels. She mentioned that her team was struggling to come up with a catchy tagline to sum up what the agency was all about.

(If you're not a marketing geek, FYI: a tagline is basically a slogan or catchphrase that's associated with a particular company. Nike's tagline is "Just do it." De Beers' tagline is "A diamond is forever.")

I mulled it over. Megan needed a new tagline for her company. I could probably whip up a couple of options for her to consider. It couldn't hurt to try, right?

I spent the next thirty minutes brainstorming a big list of tagline options. Some were pretty good, and others were seriously dumb. (Like: "Be...the belle of the brand." Um. No.)

I narrowed it down to ten really strong, catchy-sounding taglines. Then I Googled each phrase to make sure they weren't already being used by some other company. Once I felt confident that these taglines might work for Megan's company, I put together an email.

This is the exact email that I wrote:

> Subject line: Thanks! (+ Tagline Ideas)
>
> Hey Megan,
>
> I felt so energized after our chat. I love meeting entrepreneurs who are thriving (and transforming) in this murky economy.
>
> You mentioned that you might be seeking some new taglines. I came up with a couple "conservative" taglines and a couple "quirky" taglines, just for fun. I thought I'd share them with you...

Then I pasted my ten best tagline ideas, followed by:

Thanks again for meeting with me!

Megan wrote back that same day. She was impressed. She told me she'd share my tagline ideas with the rest of her team. Shortly after that, she hired me to write almost all of the language for the new company website.

"Those taglines that you wrote were better than anything we came up with on our own," she explained to me. "We really loved them."

After seeing that little sample of what I could do, she felt confident about hiring me to tackle a bigger writing project.

Just like that, I had my very first copywriting gig.

I ended up working with Megan and her company on several projects. I loved it. Every project felt like a puzzle that we got to solve with words, photos, videos, and graphics.

If a university hired us, we had to figure out how to make the school seem fun, fresh, and edgy, so that it would appeal to students, but also prestigious and valuable, so that it would appeal to their parents.

If a city tourism board hired us, we had to figure out how to make a small, quaint Midwestern town seem like the coolest vacation destination on earth.

I learned on-the-go, absorbing a huge amount of information about the marketing, branding, and advertising industry. I learned how to sum up a big idea in just a handful of words, how to stick to strict project deadlines, and how to conform to tight word limit counts and legal parameters. It was invaluable training for me. My confidence grew with each project. The team appreciated the fresh, unexpected, and occasionally super-weird ideas that I brought to the table. ("What if the debit card is like...an angel? With wings?") The whole experience catapulted my freelance writing career into a new level.

I'll always be grateful for Megan, because she gave me a shot to prove myself as a writer back when nobody knew I existed—and back when my portfolio of work was tiny and flimsy, at best.

Meeting Megan taught me that if someone says "No" or "Maybe later," that's not necessarily a firmly locked door. What they're really saying is, "Make me a better offer" or "Prove it." As in, "Prove that you're as valuable as you say you are," or "Try again—but this time, with feeling!"

I've also learned that if you contact someone to beg for a favor ("Please just give me a chance!"), then you're putting yourself into a position of neediness and desperation. Obviously, that doesn't feel good for you—or for the person you're contacting. It feels totally icky. However, if you contact someone to do a favor, or to provide an unexpected surprise, resource, or connection, then you're placing yourself in a position of generosity. You're *helping* instead of *pleading*. It feels completely different.

Megan was genuinely surprised—and impressed—by my generosity. I didn't "need" to email her a list of taglines for free. I did it because I wanted to help her out—and because I wanted to show her what I was capable of producing as a writer. And happily, it worked. One small act of generosity unlocked an exciting new job for me.

My smart friend Ellen Fondiler (you'll meet her later in this book) once said to me:

"Every door can be unlocked."

She's right. It might take a couple tries before you find the right key, but if you're persistent—and if you're a little more generous than people expect—every door can be unlocked. There's always a way to get what you want, or something pretty darn close. And often, the key to unlocking the door is *generosity*.

* * *

SURVIVAL TIP:

If you're trying to get hired, but nobody seems interested in you, ask yourself: "What's a generous, helpful, surprising thing I could do to catch their attention?"

How could you prove to them that you're seriously amazing?

Could you email a sample video to show off your video production skills—a video that your future employer could actually use to promote a new product?

Could you reach out to make a helpful referral or connection? (*"Hey, this is someone you should definitely know…"*)

Could you recommend a great resource or piece of software that might solve a problem they're having?

Could you put together a mini-proposal with five ways this company could spruce up their website or social media pages?

There are innumerable ways for you to help out, be generous, and create a bright spark in someone's day.

If one hundred people apply for the same job, but you're the *only* person who includes something "extra" that's unexpectedly generous and helpful, you are going to stand out. You're going to be the one who unlocks that door.

Plus, it just *feels* better to approach your job hunt from a place of generosity rather than desperation. You'll feel happier and lighter every time you put together a new cover letter, because you'll know that you're seriously going to brighten your recipient's day.

Chapter Two:

When Someone Writes a Terrible Review About Your Work

Gross! Really Overrated!

"Really overrated! Very small sitting area with a huge kitchen doesn't make much sense! I saw the ratings and thought it must be good, unfortunately the food was eccentric very Portland style but prepared poorly on metal plates that made me feel I was eating in a hospital. Hot chocolate was gross my kids wouldn't eat their French toast. Not very kid friendly with their $20 brunch. [. . .] I wouldn't come back."

That's the Yelp review that "Cathy S." left on April 9, 2016 shortly after visiting HunnyMilk, the brunch restaurant that my boyfriend and I started together.

(He's the chef and the mastermind behind every dish. For the first year or so, I did…everything else. I managed the dining room, greeted and served customers, handled our marketing, menu design, cleaned the bathrooms, swept up biscuits crumbs, washed dishes, and basically kept the place rolling.)

It was the first Yelp review we'd ever gotten that wasn't full of gushing, glowing praise. Every single review— prior to Cathy S.—had been "five stars."

People loved us. People raved about us. People left handwritten notes on their tables saying how amazing our food is, how they can't wait to come back again, how we're the best brunch place in town.

And then…Cathy S. shows up.

And she is profoundly unimpressed.

Reading Cathy S.'s review, I felt every imaginable emotion.

Shock.

Is this a joke? How could she possibly have had such a negative experience when all of our other customers have been so delighted?

Anger.

WTF? If she wasn't enjoying her meal, why didn't she say something? I would have happily gotten her something else. She could have spoken to me personally, rather than going onto Yelp to vent her frustrations in a public forum.

Fear.

Maybe she's right? Maybe our food is *gross*?

Confusion.

This literally makes no sense. People repeatedly tell me how much they love our food. People come back again and again to get more—and they bring their friends. How could she call our food "gross?"

Acceptance.

We live in a free country. Cathy S. is just exercising her freedom of speech. She's entitled to her own opinions, just as I am, just as everyone is.

Despair.

People are going to read Cathy S.'s review, and they'll never come to our restaurant again. We're finished. It's all over.

Curiosity.

Is there something that, maybe, we could be doing better? Maybe there's a kernel of truth to her review? Maybe we could turn this negative review into a positive opportunity? Maybe there's a lesson to be learned here?

More despair.

But it doesn't even matter because *it's all over*! We're doomed!

Standing frantically beside our kitchen table, I voiced all of these emotions to Brandon— my chef-boyfriend and business partner.

His response was:

"Whatever. It's cool. We're not for everyone."

He shrugged and returned to his mixing bowl of poppy seed bread dough.

I could not understand his reaction. He seemed so calm, relaxed, and unbothered.

"Aren't you upset? Doesn't Cathy S.'s review bother you?"

He shrugged again.

91

"Not really."

At this point my brain almost exploded. *Not really? How is that possible?*

Unlike Brandon, I feel everything with hyper-intensity. I feel other people's grief, rage, and joy like it is my own. I watch commercials for American Express credit cards, and I burst into tears. I listen to NPR, and I burst into more tears.

Being a highly sensitive, mushy-hearted, people-pleasing kind of person is both a blessing and a curse.

The blessing:

I care about people's happiness. I strive for excellence. I want everyone around me to feel comfortable at all times. I want to leave every place—and person—that I meet in better condition than I found them.

The curse:

When someone like Cathy S. shows up in my life, it temporarily destroys me. I fixate. I obsess. I replay the negative feedback over and over inside my mind, like a nightmare echo chamber. I can't let it go. Well, I can, eventually, but it takes a huge amount of effort. Unlike Brandon the Infinitely Calm Chef, it is extremely difficult for me to shrug it off and resume my dough-kneading like nothing has happened.

I admire people who have that kind of quiet inner strength and resilience.

I admire people who can face criticism—or the possibility of criticism, like stepping into an audition, or a job interview, or getting on stage—with steadiness and courage.

But how do you become that type of person?

That question began to gnaw at me. And ultimately, that's what prompted me to create this book—the one you're reading right now.

Shortly after the Cathy S. incident, I decided to reach out to a whole bunch of people—clients, friends, friends of friends, and relatives, spanning several generations and many diverse professions—to ask for true stories about criticism and discouragement.

I asked each person the same three questions:

— *Can you describe a time in your career when you felt really scared, defeated, rejected, criticized, or discouraged? What happened?*

— *What did you do to help yourself feel better?*

— *If there's someone out there who's struggling with a similar challenge or situation, what would you say to that person? What advice or words of encouragement would you give them? What do you want them to know?*

Stories poured into my inbox. Everyone had something to say—some awful memory, some cringe-worthy story, some version of "Oh my God, this happened to me..."

I found it so comforting to discover that everyone—seriously, *everyone*—struggles with criticism, rejection, and discouragement. Everyone cries into their laptop or their bowl of biscuit dough. Everyone gets upset—at least temporarily—when they get a nasty Amazon or Yelp review. Yes, even Brandon—who seems so uber-super-chill—has a few Survival Stories that would make you cringe. (In fact, you'll read one later in the book!) It's not just me. This stuff is universal. Maybe we just don't talk about it enough.

I don't feel bitter about Cathy S.'s Yelp review anymore. In fact, I feel grateful she wrote it. Because if Cathy S. hadn't left that review, then I probably wouldn't have gotten the inspiration to write this book.

Criticism has a funny way of shocking us, startling us, and crushing our egos. But criticism can also make us wiser, funnier, and more compassionate towards others.

Criticism can sting really badly. But criticism can also spark new ideas, projects, and possibilities for the future. A shockingly nasty piece of criticism could trigger an idea for your next book. Your next podcast. Your next community project. Your next song. Your bestselling memoir or documentary film.

What if that awful, gut-wrenching piece of criticism is actually a beautiful gift? I believe it's possible. I mean, it happened for me. The worst piece of criticism you can imagine...could lead to the best work you've ever done.

* * *

SURVIVAL TIP:

When you feel harshly criticized, don't isolate yourself. Reach out to your fellow human beings. Ask a friend: "Have you ever felt really criticized and rejected? What happened? How did you feel? What helped you to feel better?" Hearing other people's stories can help you feel less alone, and can bring you a much-needed perspective shift.

Don't have any friends? None at all? I'm sorry to hear that! Also, I'm guessing that's probably not true. But if there's nobody you can reach out to right this second, that's part of the reason I created this book—to share true stories about people who felt criticized, rejected, and discouraged, and how they got through it. So, please keep reading. I hope you find at least one story in this book that brings you comfort and relief.

You are not the first person to feel panicky about getting a bad Yelp review or any other tough experience like that—and you won't be the last. We're all floundering along with this stuff. You are not alone.

IT MIGHT HAVE BEEN A GOOD STORY, BUT...

Story contributed by: Maria Ross.
Author. Speaker. Founder of Red Slice, a brand consultancy.
Author of Rebooting My Brain: *How a Freak Aneurysm Reframed My Life*.

A Note from Alexandra:

Maria is one of those people who's so sparkly, so vivacious, so full of life...it's like she's got a blend of champagne and espresso flowing through her veins.

She's got gorgeous red hair, a killer smile, and she's multi-talented and successful in so many arenas—acting, speaking onstage, and running her own company, too.

When Maria told me that she's a brain injury survivor— that she almost died from a freak aneurysm, fell into a coma, and was temporary blind during her recovery period—I was dumbfounded. Seriously? I needed to hear more.

Maria has endured so much pain in her life—more than most people can imagine. Not just her brain injury—as if that's not bad enough—but other types of pain, too. Emotional pain. Criticism. Feeling misunderstood. Nasty Amazon reviews from people who (in my opinion) don't know what the hell they're talking about.

And yet, she has survived it all—with grace, humor, style, and unstoppable *joie de vivre*.

This is her story. I hope it touches your heart, just as it's touched mine. And I hope that Maria's story inspires you to call, email, or text someone you love—right now—to say, "I love you so much." Tell them now. Because our bodies are fickle machines, and life is unpredictable and strange, and tomorrow might be one day too late.

* * *

Maria: In 2008, my brain exploded.

After months of severe migraines and neck pain, an aneurysm ruptured inside my right frontal lobe. Blood hemorrhaged inside my skull. I collapsed unconscious on my bathroom floor. Luckily, since I wasn't feeling well, my husband came home early from work that day, so he was there to call the ambulance right away.

Neurosurgeons assessed the damage and performed emergency surgery. While I was lying motionless in an induced coma, the surgeons told my husband, "We've saved her life, but we have no idea of her brain damage or what she'll be like coming out of this. We've done all we can do at this point."

After emerging from the coma, I spent six weeks in the hospital recovering, while also blind because of the bleed's severity. As my vision returned—and the real work began—I saw that my long curly red hair, my trademark, had been shorn off for the surgery. I remember looking in the mirror to see this physical proof of my injury and feeling like an alien was staring back at me—like huge pieces of my identity had been torn away temporarily, or maybe forever.

While my survival was miraculous, the recovery process was slow and laborious. Things that used to feel effortless—multi-tasking, zipping speedily from project to project, remembering names, creative problem-solving, sprinting through a busy day at work, engaging in witty banter across the dinner table from my husband—felt like an immense challenge. My brain couldn't handle that kind of workload—at least, not right away. Just like it takes time for a broken bone to heal, it takes time to reboot your brain.

It was a long road. Eventually, thanks to modern medicine, therapy, patience, and a significant dose of personal moxie, I thrived and got back into my life again. But I wasn't the same woman that I'd been before. Brain injury survivors seldom are the same person afterward, even though they "look fine" on the outside. I was undeniably different and had to adapt. I had learned so many lessons about acceptance, gratitude, reinvention, and how to find humor in the darkest moments— hard-won life lessons that I felt compelled to share with others.

A few years after my aneurysm, I decided to write a memoir to share my experiences and to be a voice for those who had not recovered quite so well. Through my book, I wanted to provide hope for brain injury survivors and their families. Beyond that, I also wanted to show that intense challenges (of any kind, not just physical ones) can provide an opportunity to reframe and reboot your life. After all, when life throws you a devastating curveball, what better opportunity to ask yourself, *"What really matters to me?" "What are my real priorities?"*

"What feels like a waste of my time?" and *"How do I want to spend the remaining years of my life?"*

Injuries, illnesses, break-ups and other painful experiences can be a huge wake-up call: a golden opportunity to start living the way you've always intended. Mine certainly was.

I finished writing the book. I hired an editor to polish it up. I chose a wonderful artist to create the cover design. I self-published the book and listed it for sale on Amazon and a few other retailers. It felt like a huge personal victory to overcome my fear and share my story to help others.

And then came...the reviews.

I was blessed to receive hundreds of heartwarming reviews and private emails from people all over the world who told me how my book inspired and informed them. Some people even wrote to thank me from hospital waiting rooms, as they found my book online while a loved one was in surgery. It felt so good to know that sharing my story helped them during a very dark time.

Unfortunately, the response wasn't 100 percent positive.

Sprinkled throughout the many enthusiastic reviews, I found a smattering of negative ones. Some were vaguely uncomplimentary. Others had a "Meh, just not my thing..." tone. And a few felt quite vicious.

One reader completely misunderstood my intentions and wrote:

"It might have been a good story, but...the constant bragging about herself got old. I made it right to the point where she was talking about her beautiful hair and how people were either jealous or downright hated her for it and deleted it off of my device."

"It might have been a good story, but..." is never a terrific beginning for a book review. Ouch.

Another reader criticized my writing style, feeling it was too repetitive:

"Several items are touched upon at least twice, it becomes annoying and it makes you feel like a terrible person when you are not rooting for her but begging for the end."

Another felt, apparently, that my memoir would have been a bit more "exciting" and "suspenseful" if I had been a little closer to death:

"Interesting story well told, but not terribly exciting or suspenseful."

Another reader seemed to agree that my memoir would have been much more enjoyable and entertaining if, say, I'd had a second aneurysm or a dramatic near-death relapse of some kind:

"It started out great, a real page turner. But it bogged down after the initial life changing frenzy of the aneurysm..."

And there was one review that made me (and my husband) laugh out loud:

"It's her husband who deserves all the credit for pulling their lives back together."

Despite all the appreciation and praise, reading those few unfavorable reviews triggered all kinds of emotions.

Initially, I felt wounded and defensive—like I needed to respond publicly to each reviewer to set the record straight and convince them that their opinion was not fair or correct.

I also felt sad. Even a little heartbroken. Who wouldn't? I had poured my heart and soul and a considerable amount of time and money into creating this book. To know that a couple of people hated it—so much so, that they felt the need to publicly share just how much they hated it—well, that's an awful feeling.

How did I cope with the negative reviews?

Basically, I developed what you might call the "Pasta Strainer Method." You know when you're boiling pasta, and then you strain the water away, leaving the cooked noodles behind? That's what I tried to do with each negative review—I tried to strain away the information that was not helpful or constructive, while retaining information that could, perhaps, help me to become a better writer and storyteller in the future. For example, a couple of readers mentioned that my writing felt a bit "rambly" at times. Duly noted! That's something that I can work on. When reading reviews, my approach has become: "Keep what's helpful, ignore what's not."

When you put a creative project into the world that you care about so much—especially when it's a deeply personal topic or story—it can feel so scary to receive negative reviews. Nobody wants that.

But don't let the occasional negative comment diminish the importance of your work.

Just because one person on Amazon decides to give you a "one-star" review, that doesn't mean your project is worthless, stupid, or poorly constructed. That's just one person's opinion. What about the dozens of people who send emails to say, "Thank you for sharing your story"? What about the dozens of people who leave positive reviews? What about your friends and loved ones who share in your joy, who feel proud of you, and who encourage you and love seeing your newest work? Focus on those people. Focus on how your project is helping and influencing those lives for the better.

If you write a book, launch a website, or record a song, that's your achievement. You wrote it. You completed it. You did it. Focus on the lives you change, the impact you make, the people you help. You are allowed to feel intense pride and joy—you've earned it. A few negative reviews should not be allowed to overpower all the good you are doing for so many other people. No one can steal that joy from you unless you grant them that power.

Don't allow it. Focus on your mission and impact. Fight to protect your joy.

* * *

SURVIVAL TIP:

Negative reviews can bruise your ego. It's OK to cry, feel upset, or smack a punching bag at the gym. Do whatever you need to do. But *do not* allow negative reviews to crush your spirit.

Whatever that reviewer said, that's just one person's opinion, and you have no idea what's going on in their life. Maybe they're having an awful day. Maybe they're hungover or drunk. Maybe they just got dumped. Maybe they're jealous of the fact that you wrote a book and they didn't. Maybe they're in pain and they're lashing out in an inappropriate way. Maybe they just don't like you, period, for reasons that will never be deciphered. Who knows?

Like Maria says, focus on the people who *do* appreciate your work. Focus on the friends who support you. Focus on the clients who love you. Focus on the emails that say "Great work!" and "This really helped me!" Focus on the good work you're doing. Turn your gaze in that direction. Face yourself into the sun, not into the darkness.

SHRILL AND SHOWBIZZY.

Story contributed by: Dale Franzen.
Opera singer. Artistic director. Theater producer.

A Note from Alexandra:

This book wouldn't be complete without a Survival Story from the most inspiring woman I've ever known: my mom.

Her name is Dale. What can I tell you about Dale? Well, she's the type of mom who says to her teenage daughter, "Let's play hooky today and go to the beach!" and you're like, "Mooooom, I can't do that, I have a math test." and she's like, "Ugh, you're no fun. Life is short and in two years, that math test won't matter!" (And she's right.)

My mom has an incredible way of balancing "work" and "play." She has accomplished more than most people can even fathom. And yet, somehow, she's never too busy to drop everything and swim at the beach. Or comfort her kids. Or stop for an ice cream sundae. She's got her priorities straight.

My mom started her career as an opera singer. Later, she became a voice teacher, and after that, she raised millions of dollars to build a brand new theater. Then she "retired." One month after "retirement" (note the sarcastic quotation marks) she decided to produce a new musical that's bound for Broadway. So, now she's doing that.

Basically, my mom is my hero.

When I asked, "Hey mom, could you tell me a story about a time in your career when you felt really criticized? Like a bad review, or something like that?" she had about two hundred different stories. They're all amazing stories, and she really needs her own book. But this is the story I chose to include, because it's really funny to me, but in a sad, cringe-y kind of way.

Can you imagine getting a horrible review about your work printed in the local paper? And then all of your friends and colleagues read it? Good grief.

That happened to my mom, and this is how she survived...

* * *

Dale: You rarely remember your good reviews. But the bad ones? Those are burned into your memory forever.

The first really bad review I ever got was fairly early in my career as an opera singer.

I had gotten a supporting role in Bizet's *Carmen*. I was playing "Frasquita," a young gypsy girl who is flirtatious, adventurous, and very street-smart, issuing advice to her friend Carmen that goes ignored (with tragic consequences!).

A review came out in *The Los Angeles Times* shortly after the show opened. The reviewer praised the show and had lots of complimentary things to say about it—with one exception. He hated my performance. He called my voice "shrill and showbizzy."

"Shrill"? For a professional singer, that word is like a knife in the gut. "Showbizzy"? Not much better. I was hurt and quite shocked, because I thought I sounded great! I had no idea why this particular reviewer thought I sounded so awful, but there it was, in print, for the entire city to see.

After reading the review, I cried. My husband comforted me and insisted it wasn't true.

After crying for a while, my emotions turned from feeling hurt to feeling angry.

How dare he! Who does this reviewer think he is? Maybe he should get his hearing checked. What an idiot.

Soon, my anger subsided. I still felt slightly bitter, but I regained my composure and started to find the humor in the situation. I considered getting a t-shirt made with "SHRILL AND SHOWBIZZY" printed on the front as an inside joke for me and my closest colleagues.

While interviewing me for this book, my daughter asked me, "How did you bounce back from that negative review? How did you get over it?"

The truth is that I didn't have time to wallow and mope. I was busy! I had daily rehearsals, nightly performances, three kids at home, and I had already booked another gig that was scheduled to begin as soon as the current show's run was over. When your life is that busy, there's no time to dwell on one negative review for too long. There's just too much to do.

Many years later, by a strange twist of fate, I got offered a part in another opera—and my costar happened to be the wife of the reviewer who had called me "shrill and showbizzy" years ago. His wife and I shared a dressing room. One night, after the show, the reviewer popped back to say "hello" to his wife and he saw me sitting there, removing my makeup in front of the mirror.

"Dale!" he said warmly, as if we were old friends. "Wonderful performance. Your voice sounds fabulous, as always."

"Really?" I asked, somewhat baffled. "Because a while ago, in *The LA Times*, you wrote that my voice was 'shrill and showbizzy.'"

The reviewer gaped.

"Not possible! I never would have written that," he laughed, dismissing me with a wave of his hands. He chuckled a few times more, as if this whole thing was just a hilarious misunderstanding.

That was when I realized that reviewers are not "special." They're just ordinary people. Just like anyone else, they can be rude and careless. They can make mistakes. They don't always remember things perfectly. Their opinions are not the Word of God. Also, their opinions can change.

After that experience, I began to develop a more mature perspective on reviews—both positive and negative. Rather than celebrating (because of one good review) or sobbing (because of one bad review), I would step back and take a more holistic look at the whole situation.

I would ask myself:

—*Is the director happy with my performance?*

—*Are my castmates happy to be working with me?*

—*Is the audience responding? Are they laughing, cheering, applauding, and going on an exciting emotional ride because of my performance? Are people talking about this show, coming back to see it again, and telling all of their friends?*

—*What about my mentors and other people that I respect—what do they think about my performance?*

—*Have multiple reviews come out? What's the overall assessment of my work?*

—*Most importantly: am I proud of my performance? Do I feel like I'm giving my all?*

When you take yourself through all of those questions, then you get a well-rounded—and often, much more accurate—assessment of how you're performing and where you could improve. You can look for trends— rather than one isolated opinion.

For example, if almost every single person you speak to says "Yikes, you do sound a bit shrill" or "You sang flat on that high note" or "Your love duet doesn't feel believable; the chemistry isn't translating to the audience," then you know it's not just one person's opinion; it's a collective opinion, and it's probably something to work on.

Recently, I produced a new musical that premiered off-Broadway. Happily, the show received rave reviews from all the major publications: *The New York Times*, *Playbill*, *Variety*, even glamour magazines like *Vogue*. Obviously, the cast and production team felt thrilled to see such high praise. I was thrilled, too. But I cautioned everyone: this doesn't mean our work together is done. We still have a lot of things we can do to take this opera from good to great. We need to pay attention to musicality, the storyline of the show, audience response, ticket sales, and lots of other factors—not just the reviews.

If you're an artist, I would urge you to read your reviews—all of them, including the negative ones— because each review holds a small kernel of information about how people perceive your work. Just remember that one review is not the whole picture. To get the whole picture, you need to think holistically. Collect opinions from many sources—including your own heart and mind.

Also, if you're feeling really beaten down by negativity, take care of yourself. Get back to basics: take a long walk to empty your head, have a cup of hot tea, eat some dark chocolate, or ask a friend to come over and watch a silly movie with you. Those kinds of simple pleasures will restore your equilibrium and will remind you that your career isn't the only thing that matters in life. Your body, your family, your friends: all of these things matter and deserve your attention, too.

* * *

SURVIVAL TIP:

One positive review doesn't mean that something is "glorious and perfect." One negative review doesn't mean that something is "worthless and terrible." Reviews are just...reviews. It's one individual person's opinion. It's not the whole picture.

Like my mom, you can read all of your reviews (if you want to), but don't take any of them too seriously. And try not to obsess for days and days. As my mom learned, the person who wrote that review might not even remember writing it a few months from now. Readers probably won't remember it either.

That review might feel so devastating in this moment, and yet...life goes on. New magazines and newspapers come out. New reviews get posted. New projects get launched. People are busy. People forget and move on. You can choose to move on, too.

NUMB-NUTS.

Story contributed by: Paul Jarvis.
Designer. Software creator. Writer. Podcaster.

A Note from Alexandra:

Many years ago, I contacted Paul because I wanted to hire him to redesign my website. We started chatting about the project, discussing pricing and scheduling.

Paul told me, "Well, we'll need to get started soon, and we'll need to finish the website before the beginning of June. Because in June, I'm doing a thirty-day yoga retreat. And after that, I'm doing a road-trip with my wife. We're in a metal band together, and we're taking our van, and the pet rats, and we're heading out for a big North American tour. We'll be traveling for several months. So I won't be doing any web design projects during the summer."

Hearing all of this, I almost spluttered out my coffee. *What? Excuse me?* A 30-day yoga retreat? A metal band? With your wife?! Pet rats? Temporarily quitting your job for the entire summer, just for fun? Just because you can?

I thought to myself, *"Whoa. That is so... outrageously inspiring."*

Paul doesn't give a damn what people think about him. He works when he wants to work. He does things the way he wants. He changes his goals when he feels like it. He used to do web design, but these days, he doesn't. Instead he designs apps and teaches online classes and writes books. Paul is living Paul's Dream Life. Nobody else's.

Here's the story of how Paul survived an especially mean piece of criticism—a nasty, mean-spirited tweet from a former mailing list subscriber. Paul's response feels healthy, sane, and smart. He's one of my heroes, and I think he's about to become your new hero, too.

* * *

Paul: Every week, I send out an article that I've written to my mailing list. It's called *The Sunday Dispatches*. (TSD for short.)

Most weeks, it's just an article. Some weeks, it's an article plus an invitation to check out something I'm selling (like an app I've designed, an online course, a new book, something like that).

Every week, regardless of the topic, I get several replies (and unsubscribe messages) full of hate, anger, and general Internet vitriol.

I've been called a "spammer," a "hack," a "link-baiter," a "self-centered and flippant asshole," and a "shoddy excuse for a writer" who would do better if I stopped putting articles out.

Here's a recent gem from a man named Richard:

Like the other monetizing numb-nuts out there, you started sucking the life out of me.

Just in case Richard's message wasn't clear enough, he also tweeted at me:

@pjrvs-Hi & bye. Really enjoyed TSD-Edition No. 196. Then I wasted 2 ½ hours of my life reading your other rubbish. #Unsubscribed.

What's really amazing is that I'm not writing about religion, politics, or similar "hot button" topics. I write about freelancing, entrepreneurship, and creativity. I'm continually stunned by the level of rage that gets directed at me. It never feels good.

After receiving Richard's note, I felt sad. Sad, because I put a ton of effort into writing my article, and it was so badly received that someone felt the need to personally tell me just how much he hated it.

I did, however, appreciate Richard's use of the word "numb-nuts"—a word I haven't seen since grade school.

When someone like Richard shows up in my inbox, I have a one-day complaining rule. I'm allowed to gripe to my wife (or pet rats, both of whom are excellent listeners), whine privately to myself, and feel irritated and petty about the mean comment for one day. That's it. Then I have to move on. The "one-day rule" works for me—it gives me time to vent, but doesn't let me dwell on anything too long. (I'm also typically too busy creating or writing new material to focus on any one piece of hate for too long.)

Criticism does affect me. I'm human. I have feelings, and I feel deeply about what I put out into the world.

But I learned—ages ago—that I can't let that type of negative criticism guide or stop my work. If a single person's hatred of art was all that was required to stop it, we'd have no music, writing, painting, or anything at all. Progress—as a creative person—is impossible if we let our fears dictate our actions and our art.

In some ways, I like that certain folks hate what I do. It means that my line in the sand is evident, and that my opinions are coming through clearly.

Creativity requires a willingness to take risks. Every time I write, design, teach, share advice, give things away for free, or sell something, I know I am taking a risk. It's the risk of criticism, hate, and judgment—but then, on the flip side, there's also the opportunity to connect, change, and, most importantly, to help someone.

One day—out of the blue—I received an email from a substance abuse counselor who wanted to know if she could share an article that I wrote with her group of people in recovery. It's an article that I've been told "brings nothing to the table" and "is a waste of words." It was a business article, but she said it felt very relevant to the recovery process because it discussed the commitment of giving your word. Seeing her note made my entire day.

That's the funny thing about sharing your creative work.

You write an article. Someone like Richard thinks you're a "numb-nuts" (and tells you so). But then, across the country, sitting at some other desk, someone else reads that same article and thinks, *"This is beautiful. I need to share this with everyone I know."*

I am driven to create for the people who like what I'm doing—and want more.

Knowing that those people exist is what inspires me to keep clicking "publish" and "send."

* * *

SURVIVAL TIP:

If you get a bad review from a reader, client, customer, audience member, or newsletter subscriber, it's never a fun experience. But try to remember that one person's opinion doesn't necessarily mean your work is "bad." Different people have different opinions and preferences. That's just the way the world works.

Person A might taste your food and think, *"Gross! Way too sweet. Disgusting."*

Person B might taste your food and think, *"Delicious! I've got a major sweet tooth and I'm literally in heaven. This is the best."*

No matter what you're creating, and no matter how much love, care, and thoughtfulness you pour into your work, it is impossible to please everybody on the entire planet.

There's always going to be someone who loves what you're doing, and someone who doesn't. It's annoying, but it's something we all have to accept.

Tell yourself, *"I can't control how people react to my work. All I can do is try to be helpful, and try to do a good job, and try to send love and positivity into the world. How that 'love' gets interpreted...that's not within my control."*

People will always have their opinions. Channel your inner Paul Jarvis, and just keep doing your thing.

YOU'RE WASTING YOUR LIFE.

Story contributed by: L'Erin Alta.
Spiritual teacher. Scribe. Shadow diver.

Note from Alexandra:

The first time I met L'Erin, I felt like I was encountering
an extraterrestrial being from another planet. Or maybe
another universe. She's one of those people who is so
serene, so grounded, and so strikingly beautiful—inside
and out—that you basically do a double-take. *"Whuh-
whuhhh? Is that, like...a human being? It can't be."*

Describing L'Erin's career is difficult, because she
doesn't fit into any clear-cut boxes. She doesn't have
a straightforward one-word job title like "surgeon" or
"hairstylist." She contains multitudes.

L'Erin is a spiritual teacher. She's a writer. She's a
workshop facilitator. She's a modern-day medicine
woman who helps people grieve, heal from trauma,
and move forward with their lives. Also, she owns a
tutu (more than one, possibly?), and she has the *best*
earrings. Basically, she's a magical being.

But when your job description doesn't fit neatly onto
the front of a business card, it can be tough out there.
People might not understand you. Your parents might
feel confused. Even your closest friends might struggle to
introduce you at parties. "Oh, have you met L'Erin? She's
amazing. She does...ah, um, L'Erin? What is it that you
do, exactly?"

L'Erin knows what it feels like to be "different" and "difficult to categorize." She's encountered so many people who don't understand her work—or worse, who strongly disapprove of her career.

I asked L'Erin to share a piece of her story, because I admire the way that she's forging ahead with her career regardless of what people think or say. Negative reviews. Negative comments. It doesn't matter. L'Erin keeps L'Erin-ing along.

It takes tremendous courage to do that—and I hope L'Erin's story helps you feel a little more courageous, too.

The world needs surgeons and hairstylists, certainly. But the world also needs mystics, medicine women, shamans, healers, and un-boxable magical beings, too.

* * *

L'Erin: Everyone expected me to attend a prestigious college, earn a degree with top honors, and enter the workforce along with my briefcase and pantsuit. Education. Law. Finance. Some type of respected profession that would make my years of hard work worth the investment.

Instead, I dropped out of school and spent fifteen years traveling the world—visiting twenty-three different countries, living with indigenous communities, studying different types of rituals, healing arts, and spiritual traditions—and living the gypsy nomad lifestyle.

One day, in the midst of my international travels, I got a phone call from a man that I've known my entire life. We aren't related by blood, but he has always felt like a brother to me. We grew up together, and he's as close to "family" as it gets.

"We are very worried about you," he told me. "We" as in—him and the folks back home, my classmates and friends I'd grown up with.

He explained that he didn't approve of my choices, that he felt I was "escaping adulthood" by traveling instead of going back to finish college. He wanted to know what I was "running away" from, why I couldn't just choose a normal career and "settle down."

"You're wasting your life," he said solemnly.

I thought he was joking—or at least partially joking. I actually giggled in response. I was having the most incredible life—seeing the world, traveling to places that most people only dream about—surely he knew that!

Surely he was kidding around. Surely he couldn't mean all of those things he'd just said. Surely he wasn't actually "worried" about me. That just didn't seem possible.

It took several years—and several more conversations—before I realized he wasn't kidding at all. He was dead serious. He really thought I was wasting my life.

Almost everyone from my old community back home—all the friends I'd grown up with—had followed in our parents' footsteps and pursued conventional careers.

They were MBAs and lawyers, PhDs and corporate ladder climbers. And me? I was doing Ayahuasca ceremonies with shamans...having a private audience with the Dalai Lama...spending the night on the Great Wall of China...surviving avalanches in the Himalayas... and earning my certification to work as both a yoga teacher and birth doula. I was the lone freak-wolf who had separated from the rest of the pack.

The realization dawned on me: although my mom generally had my back, my family of origin no longer approved of me. In fact, they were deeply disappointed in me. It was like they couldn't "see" me. They couldn't see the amazing person I knew I was becoming. All they could see was the "proper," "correct" path that I hadn't chosen to take. I felt misunderstood and invisible.

My place in the community that I had long cherished— sister, friend, confidante, peer—no longer seemed to fit.

While some people celebrated my adventurous spirit, their compliments were laced with whispers of being secretly jealous, and most of them still saw me as an outlier in comparison to their upwardly mobile lives. Not being valued as a peer was difficult to accept, and it stung for a really long time.

One thing that did help me, though, was trying to look at the situation from my friend's perspective.

He'd grown up in a family haunted by financial instability. As a result, he grew up with a gnawing hunger for security and wealth that looked like home ownership, graduate degrees, a six-figure income, a nice car, and other conventional markers of success. To him, those things represented "a good life." That's how he sees the world. So it makes sense that he would look at my choices and think, "She's doing it wrong. She's wasting her life."

Considering my friend's upbringing and value system helped me to feel less "invisible." I could understand his perspective. I didn't necessarily agree with him—but I could understand why he felt the way he felt and why he said the things he said.

My friend is still part of my life and probably always will be. He still doesn't see me as a viable adult, but I've learned that...that's OK. He doesn't need to approve of my choices in order for me to love my life. I stamp my own parking validation ticket here on planet Earth. I approve of myself.

Despite what some people may think, I know that I am not "wasting my life."

Quite the opposite.

I have created a life that includes self-employment, freedom, flexibility, and absolutely zero briefcases, pantsuits, or blazers with shoulder pads. I never have to punch a timecard. I never have to plead with my boss for a raise or extra time off. I have the ability to work when I want to and how I want to (often with my dog curled up in my lap). Later this year, I am traveling to Iceland and Africa to lead women's retreats on healing, sacred storytelling, and dance. My career feels like a creative playground. My time is my own.

Wasting my life? No.

I am creating my own version of paradise.

* * *

SURVIVAL TIP:

Sometimes criticism comes in the form of a review posted on Yelp, Amazon, or in the local newspaper. Other times, criticism comes in a different form—like an email from an editor, client, or boss, or a comment from a family member or friend. It could be a friend who doesn't approve of your career, and who tries to convince you to "get a real job."

If that happens to you, try not to become defensive. If you get angry and start justifying your choices, that's unlikely to make things better.

Instead, try to stay calm. Just like L'Erin, try to figure out what's compelling this person to make these kinds of comments. Are they worried you won't be able to make a living? Are they concerned about your physical safety? Perhaps you can provide some comfort by saying, "You know, I really love my career, and I'm doing great. I've got clients that I love, and projects that excite me. You don't need to worry about me."

You can also say...nothing. Just carry on. Do your thing. Not everyone will "get" what you're doing. Some people will be ecstatic to RSVP for your party, and some people won't. You've got to keep throwing your kind of party.

Make life feel like your own personal version of paradise, and enjoy every moment.

Chapter Three:

When Your Boss, Client, or Customer Is Totally Disappointed

IS THAT ALL YOU GOT?

Story contributed by: Brandon Weeks.
Chef and owner of HunnyMilk, a brunch restaurant.

A Note from Alexandra:

I met Brandon online. More specifically—an online dating website called OKCupid. Yup. As you've probably gathered from some of the earlier stories in this book, Brandon is my sweetheart. My true love. My best friend. The first person I see every morning. The last person I see every night. The man who occasionally encourages me, very sweetly and gently, to stop typing in my filthy yoga clothes and maybe, you know, take a shower.

We connected on the Internet, bonded over our mutual love of cheese, chocolate, and croissant dough, and after our very first date—that was it. We've been together ever since.

Brandon has been a professional chef for over ten years. He's one of those quiet types who doesn't like to brag about his professional accomplishments. So I'll do the bragging for him...

Brandon has worked at some of the top restaurants in the country. He's been named one of the "best chefs in Portland" and his brunch restaurant has been called one of the "top brunches in America." He's been written up in *Newsweek*, *Time Out*, and lots of other places. One time, my friend Nicole popped into his restaurant, and Brandon's food was so good that she started moaning

125

and slamming her fork down in hysterics, saying, "I want to keep eating this…until I die."

So, that gives you an idea of what Brandon's all about. (And yes—I'm aware that I'm a very, very lucky woman. How many ladies have a partner who brings home industrial-sized vats of Nutella? Or who whips up Bakewell tarts and Beef Wellington and homemade potato gnocchi on an ordinary Tuesday night, just 'cause? Not many.)

Of course, Brandon didn't always run his own restaurant, and he didn't always get high praise in the media. Back in the early days of his culinary career, he was just a lowly kitchen scrub, doing his best not to screw everything up. This is one of my favorite stories from Brandon's early career, and I think you'll love it, too…

* * *

Brandon: Shortly after graduating from culinary school, I was fortunate enough to get a job working at Charlie Trotter's in Chicago.

Trotter's is no longer in operation. It closed shortly before the owner's death in 2012. However, years ago, back when I worked there, it was one of the most acclaimed, celebrated restaurants in America.

Getting hired to work at Trotter's was an honor. Not getting immediately fired was an honor. Having "Trotter's" on your résumé was something that many chefs, like me, coveted. It was a golden stamp of approval that could unlock doors for you in the future.

But in order to earn that golden stamp of approval, first you had to prove yourself—and that wasn't easy to do.

Trotter's was a hellish, intense, military-like atmosphere. I typically worked sixteen hours a day—for minimum wage—in an atmosphere where even the smallest mistake was not tolerated. I would show up. Work. Go home. Sleep a few hours. Head back. Start the cycle all over again. Many of the chefs pounded cans of Red Bull or even snorted cocaine in the bathrooms just to stay awake.

It was brutal. I had no social life or "me time" whatsoever—but at that early stage in my career, the sacrifice felt "worth it." It was invaluable training for a young chef like me, because I got to work shoulder-to-shoulder with some of the best living chefs in the world.

One of those chefs was a guy named Matthias Merges. He was my hero and unofficial mentor.

I guess Matthias saw a sliver of potential in me, because—a few months after getting hired at Trotter's—he gave me a special task to complete. He asked me to prepare a selection of *mignardises*, which are miniature pastries and candies typically served with coffee just after dessert, or boxed up with a fancy ribbon to take home as a farewell treat for the restaurant patrons.

I specialized in pastries at culinary school, so I figured, *"I got this."*

The next day, Matthias walked into the kitchen and asked to see my *mignardises*. I showed him three tiny

127

pastries. Three totally different flavors. A cute little trio of sweets.

"Is that all you got?" he asked.

His tone was so flat and unimpressed. My stomach sank into my feet. I knew, immediately, that he had expected so much more from me. His comment felt like a slap in the face.

That same day, I put in extra time after my shift and developed four more options.

The following day, I proudly presented Matthias with seven different *mignardises*—more than double what I'd delivered the previous day.

This time, he nodded approvingly. His facial expression read, *"That's more like it."*

That's how I began to earn Matthias' respect.

Many years later, I visited a new restaurant in Las Vegas that Matthias started called Yusho. I emailed Matthias a few days beforehand to mention that I'd be coming by. He wasn't there that night, but he instructed his staff to make my meal "on the house" and to send out all kinds of extra treats, like mochi balls filled with ice cream. It was such a generous gesture. I felt amazed that Matthias remembered me after all these years. That felt like the highest compliment, especially from such a discerning chef.

Way back on that day when Matthias criticized my *mignardises*, I felt awful and ashamed. But looking back,

I am grateful he gave me that *"Seriously? That's it?"* tone of voice, because it motivated me to do better.

If everyone smiles and praises you constantly, regardless of your actual performance, that's not particularly helpful. Sometimes, a small jab can provoke you to reach higher and put forth your best work.

Today, I run my own restaurant, and I have a terrific staff. Sometimes, though, I notice sloppy errors—items not plated properly, sauces running together when they ought to be separate, too much mousse, not enough strawberries, and so on. In those moments, I try to intervene immediately and give constructive criticism on the spot. This is what restaurateur Danny Meyer calls "correcting with dignity"—correcting someone's mistake without screaming or getting hysterical, offering criticism while still allowing your employee to keep his or her dignity intact. Hopefully, by doing this, I can become someone else's "Matthias" and help to elevate their quality of work.

If Matthias had not criticized me way back then, who knows? Maybe I'd still be under-performing and dishing out three pastry options when I have the capacity to create so much more. Criticism is not always a terrible thing. Sometimes criticism can be a gift that's wrapped in a somewhat prickly, uncomfortable package.

* * *

SURVIVAL TIP:

If a client or boss criticizes your work, your first instinct might be to curl up in a tight little ball and quietly die. Or you might feel defensive, and think to yourself, *"Well, screw them! I'm awesome. They're stupid."*

Yes, you are definitely awesome. However, there might be a kernel of truth contained in this piece of criticism. There might be something you can learn or improve upon.

Open yourself up to the possibility that maybe, possibly, you could hone your skills a bit further, or push yourself a little harder. Are you really giving your best effort—or more like a 25% effort? Be honest with yourself. This type of honesty is what propels your work from "pretty good" to "phenomenal."

I Don't Like Any of It.

Back when I was getting started as a self-employed writer, I was haunted with anxieties about money...pretty much nonstop.

I'd stare at my bank account balance and feel a thick, twisty knot of dread in the pit of my stomach. Then I'd stare into my (almost empty) inbox and wonder, *"When are clients going to start emailing me? Why does it feel like nobody knows that I exist?"*

In those early days, on the rare occasions when a potential client emailed me, I would think: *"OMG.*

Hallelujah! Sweet baby Jesus! Christmas in a basket!"
I'd leap at the opportunity without asking any questions.
I was so grateful to have any money flowing in. If a
potential client asked me to jump, I'd ask, "How high?"
before asking, "Uh, so, who are you exactly?"

My tendency to say, "Yes! I'm available! When can we
start?" ultimately got me into some trouble. Because
when you're saying "Yes!" to every invitation that you
receive—without any kind of vetting process—you're
going to wind up with quite a few projects that aren't
a good fit for your skills. And this mismatch can be
absolutely exhausting—for you, and for your client, too.

One of my very first clients was a consultant who needed
to revamp her website. She primarily did leadership
coaching, seminars, and other types of team-building
work for big corporations. We spoke briefly. She was
smart, passionate, and perfectly lovely.

However, something in my gut whispered to me, *"She's
great, but I'm probably not the ideal writer for this
project. She's looking for someone who writes in a very
corporate-sounding way, and that's just not me."*

I decided to ignore this gut feeling. She liked me, and I
liked her, and I definitely needed the money, so I said,
"I'd love to work with you!"

She asked me to re-write all of her website language and
make everything sound even more clear and impressive.
She also wanted me to rewrite her LinkedIn profile, her
media kit, and a few other marketing materials as well.

It was a hefty bundle of work. And she was happy to pay me upfront.

"Hmm, I don't know about this..." my gut whispered again. I brushed these feelings aside like muffin crumbs off a table.

"Sounds great!" I told my new client. "I'm so excited to get started!"

We dove in. I interviewed her over the phone. I took copious notes. I spent hours poring over her website and watching her videos to familiarize myself with her work. I wrote pages of new material. Certain paragraphs took me hours—an absurd length of time— because I wanted everything to be "just right." I proofread everything with extreme care and triple-checked every sentence. It was a ton of work, and in the end, I felt proud of how everything turned out. I attached all of the documents to an email, sent it over, and crossed my fingers.

"I hope she loves it," I thought.

Spoiler alert: she did not love it.

It took several days for her to get back to me. Finally, she asked if we could talk on the phone.

"I don't exactly know how to say this," she began hesitantly, "But I don't like any of it."

My mind went blank. My throat went dry. *"I don't like any of it."* What? Huh? Does not compute. I had worked so hard on this project—extra-double-super hard. She'd paid me for about ten hours of work, and in reality, I'd put in about twenty-five to thirty hours. Maybe more.

I asked her to elaborate. She struggled to find the words.

"I don't know, exactly. It's hard to explain. I just doesn't sound like I hoped it would. Something's not right."

I could tell she was trying to be polite and respectful, but her voice sounded strained. This wasn't an easy conversation for her, or for me. It was totally awkward. She had already paid me upfront for the entire project. She was on a tight deadline to relaunch her website. And now she had pages of language that she didn't like and couldn't use. Total nightmare.

I wanted to evaporate and disappear from the face of the earth because the whole thing felt so embarrassing. I felt like an absolute failure.

"Now what?" I wondered to myself.

What's the protocol? What do we do next? Start over from scratch? Try to rework what we've already got? Part ways? Refer her to another writer? Give her a refund? Something else?

I had already invested so much time and energy into this project. Starting over felt like an exhausting option. But ultimately, that's what we decided to do.

We began fresh. Another phone call. Another round of writing. Total do-over.

The second time around, things went a bit better. Not an immediate slam-dunk, but not awful. We finessed and tweaked things back and forth for several days. Eventually, after multiple rounds of re-writing and revising, she felt satisfied.

It wasn't exactly a flowing, effortless collaboration—but eventually, we got the job done.

I exhaled a huge sigh of relief once that project was officially over. Then I tried to unpack everything that had gone wrong, because I definitely didn't want to repeat that type of experience again.

After chewing things over for several days, I admitted to myself, *"I had a gut feeling about this project, and I ignored it. That was obviously a mistake. Just because someone is interested in hiring me, that doesn't necessarily mean I should say 'Yes'. If my gut says 'No', I need to trust that instinct and refer them to somebody else."*

When you're self-employed, it can feel absolutely crazy to turn away a potential client. You might think, *"I can't afford to turn anybody away! Refer them to someone else? That's bonkers!"*

But it's not bonkers. It's actually very wise. Being more selective can help you avoid dozens of sleepless, anxious nights, save you hundreds of hours of wasted time, and protect you from unhappy situations, refund requests, and all of that icky stuff that you definitely don't want.

Over the years, I've learned to trust what I call my "hut" (heart + gut).

Whether you're job hunting, trying to line up clients, or considering any other kind of invitation or opportunity, I urge you to trust your hut, too.

If you're getting a funny red-flag feeling that's purely emotional and doesn't seem to make any rational sense, just go with it. *Trust your hut.* You'll be happier. Your clients will be happier, too. Your projects will flow along more smoothly. You'll do better quality work. People will rave about you. Your reputation will be golden. And in the long run, you'll earn more money, too.

In work, and in the rest of your life, when your hut starts talking to you, pay attention. Your hut knows what's up.

* * *

SURVIVAL TIP:

The next time someone says, "I want to hire you," take a few minutes to assess the situation before you immediately say, "Great! Let's go!"

Before saying "Yes," ask yourself:

—Does this project sound interesting to me? Does it sound fun? Inspiring? Rewarding?

—What, if anything, do I know about this person? What's their deal? Where's their website? What's their

mission? What are they all about? Are they an axe-murderer? Etc.

—Is this person asking for a type of service that I don't really provide, or something that's out of my skill set, or something that bores me? Is there another service provider—maybe even a friend of mine—who might be a better fit for this project?

(You can use these kinds of questions when you're freelancing, but also when you're searching for a more traditional nine-to-five job, too.)

If you need more info, email the potential client (or employer) and ask a few questions. Or set up a phone call. After collecting more information, check in with yourself and see if you have an instinctive feeling about this opportunity.

What is your hut (heart + gut) telling you about this project, client, or company? Does your hut think that it's going to be amazing—or stressful and unrewarding?

Personally, my hut is always 100 percent correct. It's eerily accurate. Yours probably is, too. Please do not ignore your hut.

OOPS! MY CLIENT IS A DRUG LORD.

Story contributed by: Theresa Reed.
Tarot card reader. Astrologer. Author of *The Tarot Coloring Book*.

A Note from Alexandra:

I used to be somewhat skeptical about oracles, astrologers, and people who shuffled Tarot decks for a living. That is...until I met Theresa.

Theresa is the cool, business-savvy auntie that you've always wanted. She's freakishly intuitive, hysterically funny, a consummate professional, and one of the hardest workers I've ever met.

She's been a professional Tarot card reader for nearly thirty years. Her clients include police officers, hairdressers, soccer moms, celebrities, and just about everyone in between. Once you get a Tarot reading with Theresa, you will be *hooked*. She doesn't just reveal exciting possibilities for your future—she really makes you believe in yourself, and believe in your own power to transform, take charge, and take your life in any direction you want. She always tells her clients: "The cards tell a story, but *you* write the ending." Mysticism with a dose of personal responsibility? Count me in.

Given her unconventional career, Theresa has some of the weirdest, wildest, scariest, spookiest Survival Stories I've ever heard. It was challenging to narrow it down and decide which one to put into this book! This one's a real winner, though. I can almost guarantee—no matter how bad things get with your career, you're probably *never* going to have a workday as terrible as this one...

* * *

Theresa: Twenty years ago, I got booked to do a Tarot party. That's where a client hires me to set myself up at a table—usually at a house party—and read Tarot cards for all the guests in attendance. I packed my favorite deck, got all dolled up, and drove over to the house where the party was already underway.

The moment I walked inside, I realized that I'd walked straight into a scene out of the movie *Training Day*. (If you've never seen that movie, Google it. Especially the scene with Ethan Hawke in the bathtub.)

Everyone in the house was a gang member—or a gang member's girlfriend. I mean...*everyone*.

Everyone was packing a gun, a knife, and Lord only knows what else. The vibe was seedy and terrifying. I almost bolted out the door, but I was worried that someone would drag me right back inside! I swallowed, steadied myself as best I could, and held my head up high.

I've lived in some pretty gritty parts of the country, and I knew the worst thing I could do was look "scared." I needed to project an aura of confidence, even if I was shaking in my Doc Martens.

The gang leader—aka my distinguished client—
positioned himself in front of me, across the
kitchen table.

He had his entire crew surrounding him. He stared
at me with dead, oily eyes and told me he wanted a
Tarot reading.

His first question?

"Which of my boys can I trust?"

Uh oh.

I shuffled my deck and his gang members stared at
me with looks of terror. It was obvious that if I said
the wrong thing, or indicated that any of them were
untrustworthy, these boys were going to be escorted
from the party and deposited into the river with bricks
tied around their ankles. Their lives were riding on
whatever I said next.

I turned over each card and delivered my reading
calmly and professionally—for my own protection
as well as everyone else's. I chose my words with
exceptional caution.

Once the reading was over, the gang leader looked
satisfied—and his buddies exhaled sighs of relief. I got
paid—cash, obviously—and made my way for the door,
still calm and cool as a cucumber. The moment I got
home? *Total freak-out.* I screamed into a pillow, dry-
heaved, cried, and uncorked all of the stress I'd been
holding inside.

After that, I became a lot more cautious and protective with every aspect of my business. Personal phone number? Only for trusted insiders. Home address? Definitely not going on my website. In-person Tarot readings? Only for a select few.

I wised up really quick and I stopped putting myself into dangerous situations. No amount of money is worth putting your safety or sanity at risk.

To this day, I have extremely strict policies and boundaries with my clients, and I'm very selective about who I allow into my "inner circle." Drug lords? No thank you, ma'am. I'm just grateful that my drug lord client was satisfied with my work, because if he wasn't, that party could have taken a really dark turn. And I'd be swimming with the fishes.

I truly hope that you *never* find yourself accidentally working for a mafia kingpin. Try to avoid that if you can. However: at some point or another, you're probably going to find yourself in a really distressing workplace situation. It might not be gang-related. But it might be a supervisor who doesn't respect you. Or a colleague who verbally abuses you. Or an overly-dramatic client who makes every single minuscule detail feel like a life-and-death situation, even if that's far from the truth. Your success will be defined by how you react in those situations. Will you cower? Will you run for the door? Will you take action to make things right? Will you maintain your cool? Most importantly: Will you protect yourself?

Whether you're a Tarot reader, a delivery truck driver, a high school teacher, or a parole officer, you've got to take steps to protect yourself at work, emotionally and physically. Hope for the best, but be prepared for the worst case scenario. And if your new client is packing heat, just say whatever he wants you to say, bow politely, and then get the heck outta there. Because you do *not* want to end up in that *Training Day* bathtub.

* * *

SURVIVAL TIP:

Considering a new job or project? Ask around. Find out if this company—or client—is great to work with, or a high-maintenance diva, or a monster, or, you know, a murderous drug lord. Never hurts to do some research and double-check.

And if you ever feel unsafe in a workplace situation, get out of there as quickly as you can. Your mental and physical safety must *always* be the top priority. File an official complaint or report, if needed. Take precautions in the future to prevent this type of scenario from ever happening again. Your life has no price tag, so please never prioritize "making a few bucks" above your safety.

Lastly: take comfort in the fact that your "worst boss ever" will probably be a cherubic angel compared with Theresa's gangster client! If your boss is behaving rudely or being unreasonable, well, at least you'll know...it could be a lot worse.

HOW COULD THIS HAPPEN?

Story contributed by: Melinda Massie.
Professional Organizer. Founder of A Side of Fabulous.

A Note from Alexandra:

I have a confession: I am obsessed with cleaning, decluttering, and organizing.

The Life-Changing Magic of Tidying Up by Marie Kondo is basically my Holy Bible. I rummage through our clothes, drawers, cabinets, bookshelves, and storage bins on a monthly basis, and I'm continually finding new ways to spruce up our home.

This habit of mine drives Brandon slightly insane, because I'm constantly putting his things in "surprising, exciting new places." But he likes it when I vacuum and mop. No complaints about that. In fact, he bought me an industrial-style mop bucket for my birthday last year—the bright yellow kind with the gigantic bucket on wheels. Absolute heaven! I woke up at 5:00 a.m. on my birthday and mopped the entire apartment until it was surgically clean. OK, now you know *waaay* more about me than you ever needed to.

My point is, when Melinda offered to contribute a story for this book, I felt extremely excited. Because Melinda is a professional organizer. That's my secret dream job!

Melinda shared her Survival Story with me via email, and it's a perfect example of how to deal with an unhappy client or boss in a dignified manner—and how to conduct yourself with tact and professionalism. (Even if you're freaking out on the inside.)

* * *

Melinda: When someone inquires about hiring me, I always explain my services very, very clearly to prevent any misunderstanding or disappointment later down the line.

First, I explain that I'm a "professional organizer"— which is not the same thing as a "housekeeper." I can help you sort through your clothes, declutter your office, unpack all of those long-forgotten boxes in your attic, and help you decide which possessions to keep and which to release—but I'm not going to scrub the toilet or mop the kitchen floor.

Second, I always make sure to explain that organizing is a collaborative process. It's a team effort. My client and I need to work side-by-side, spend time together, communicate openly, and make decluttering decisions together. I can't dive in by myself and decide what stays in someone else's home and what's got to go. I need my client to participate in the process, or it's not going to work.

Most of my clients totally get it. We dive in, get to work, and the results are spectacular! But once in a while, a client comes along who forgets—or ignores—the guidelines that I've laid out. This doesn't happen often, but when it does, it's incredibly stressful.

I'll never forget one client who hired me about two years after I started my organizing business.

During our first work session, we focused on decluttering her office. We purged tons of unnecessary items and gave the space a pretty significant makeover. At the end of our session, I asked how she felt about the work we'd gotten done. She said she felt good. She scheduled our next appointment on the spot and wrote me a check.

The next day, I sent a follow-up email telling her how much I enjoyed working with her, congratulating her on the work done so far, reminding her about her homework (I always give my clients small assignments to work on in between our appointments) and giving a few other tips. I also mentioned that I was looking forward to our next appointment. She didn't respond.

The following week—on the morning of our next scheduled appointment—I finally got a reply from my client. She told me that she hated my work, hated my style of organizing, and was so upset and disappointed that she had canceled the check she gave to me. She said she had already hired a different organizer, and she wouldn't require my services any longer. But then towards the bottom of her email, she said she felt sorry for canceling the original check, and she would go ahead and send me another one.

I read this woman's email with my jaw hanging open and my heart pounding wildly.

What on *Earth*?

I felt so many emotions.

I was hurt that she didn't like my work. (And if she didn't like my work, why had she told me everything was "good" only to send a furious email a week later?)

I was saddened that she'd kept her feelings bottled inside—and that she didn't feel she could be honest with me face to face.

I was angry that she had waited to cancel her second appointment until just a few hours before it was scheduled to begin. She lived over an hour away, so I had cleared my entire day to go visit her. It felt very disrespectful to get such a last-minute cancelation.

I was pissed that she had canceled the check out from under me. Another disrespectful blow. (But then she decided to send me another check to replace the canceled one? Huh? Totally erratic and bizarre.)

Most of all, I was terrified that she was going to leave a nasty review online. I was so terrified about this that I apologized profusely (even though I didn't think I had done anything wrong) and gave her a 50 percent discount on the fee for our initial work session in the hope that she wouldn't say anything bad about me online. (Thankfully, she didn't.)

The whole situation was emotionally exhausting. I had never experienced anything like it up until that point—or since, for that matter.

For days afterward, I ran through every minute detail in my head:

Did I fail to explain my services accurately and clearly?

Did I do something awful to offend her without realizing it?

Did I misread her emotions while we were working together?

Is she severely depressed or mentally unstable in some way?

Most of my clients enjoy working with me—how could something like this happen?

I hashed it all out in my head. I described the whole saga and vented to a close friend. I soothed myself with Netflix episodes, a few cocktails, and probably something fried and/or covered in creamy gravy. (I don't remember exactly what I ate, but I am pretty sure gravy was involved.)

Eventually, I calmed down and came to the realization that this woman's response (probably) had very little to do with me. She was evidently going through a very difficult chapter in her life—and apparently she was struggling to express her feelings honestly. Something about our work together "triggered" her and caused her to lash out in anger.

Was it my fault? I don't think so. I was not the real source of the problem. I just happened to be the trigger that sent her over the edge.

This has been a lesson I have continually learned, and re-learned, throughout my life and career. If a client is screaming at you, if someone is honking their car horn obnoxiously, if you get a furious email from someone threatening to cancel a check, who knows why this person is behaving this way?

Maybe her husband just walked out, and she's panic-stricken and seething with anger.

Maybe his wife just passed away, and he needs somewhere to vent his grief and rage.

Maybe she's hungry, tired, or cranky due to a severe headache! Who knows?

There are so many reasons why people behave cruelly, erratically, and insensitively. It might be directly related to you, it might be vaguely related to you, or it might have absolutely nothing to do with you.

It's unfortunate, but sometimes you get caught in the crossfire of someone else's bad day. That's just the reality of living on a crowded planet filled with seven billion people, all of whom are going through their own personal experiences, challenges, joys, sorrows, and disappointments.

Sometimes other people's emotions splatter onto you, and it's messy and unpleasant. But you will survive.

It's helpful to remember that even situations that feel absolutely horrendous—like having a client declare they "hated" working with you—are always temporary.

Thunderstorms pass. Life goes on. One furious client will not unravel your career.

Breathe, eat some gravy, do some yoga, and keep marching forward.

* * *

SURVIVAL TIP:

At least once in your career, you're probably going to have a client, colleague, or boss who is totally unsatisfied with your work, and who's nasty and bitter and awful about it, and...it might have *nothing* to do with you.

They might be hungry. They might be tired. They might have a migraine. They might be dealing with extreme stress at home, or intense pressure from their own boss.

Breathe. Remain calm. Pretend like you're a flight attendant dealing with a hysterical passenger. Be compassionate, yet firm. Try to resolve the situation as best you can. Offer a packet of salted peanuts. (Maybe they have low blood sugar? It couldn't hurt!)

Then, as Melinda recommends, just move on. Keep marching forward. Hopefully, it won't happen again. But if it happens repeatedly, consider moving on to a new job, or a new client. Because you're not supposed to be a hysterical person's punching bag day after day. You deserve better treatment than that.

I'M GOING TO HELL.

Story contributed by: [Prefers to be unnamed].
Attorney.

A Note from Alexandra:

This attorney asked to remain anonymous to preserve his clients' privacy. But he generously shared this story with me—and while it's short, it's packed with wise guidance.

We met for cappuccinos in Los Angeles, and he described a few of the craziest moments from his thirty-year career. I deeply admire anybody who has the courage to stand up and speak in front of a judge and jury. I'm pretty sure I'd buckle under that type of pressure. My courtroom presentation would be something like: "Hi guys, um, so, allow me to present Exhibit A. Actually, I meant Exhibit B. Actually, whoops, that's a photo of some pretty latte art from the other day. It was supposed to be a picture of...you know what? Never mind. The other guy wins. Byeeeee!"

Being a successful lawyer requires the patience of a saint and nerves of steel. And when you've got a challenging case *plus* a client who's having a hysterical meltdown right in the courtroom? Whoa. It's not easy to keep your cool.

If you have a boss, client, or colleague at work who flips out over the smallest things—people who overreact, people who send emails marked *urgent* fifteen times a day, people who worry, fret, stress, and micromanage your work because they're convinced everything's going to fall apart—then this story will probably feel very familiar to you.

Of course, even when you've got colleagues who behave atrociously, it's still possible to do your job with grace and composure—just like the attorney you're about to meet. Yes, you can conduct yourself like a professional, even when everybody else is behaving like a sleep-deprived toddler. It's not easy, but it's possible.

* * *

[Prefers to be unnamed]: As an attorney, you must remain calm and professional even when a crisis is erupting right in front of your eyes.

One time, a client broke down during a failed mediation session and moaned, "I'm going to hell."

He was exhausted and distraught. The comment wasn't directed at me, but of course I felt terrible, like I had failed him in some way.

Whether you're an attorney or an architect or an engineer, nobody ever wants to see a client on the verge of tears.

(In the end, we settled the case, and everything turned out fine. He didn't go to "hell"—in fact, he was awarded millions of dollars. Even so, I vividly remember that mediation session and the anguished expression on my client's face. It was a bleak moment. I'll never forget it.)

Another time, in the middle of a trial, a client of mine became overwhelmed with emotion and couldn't stop herself from exploding with outbursts like "Liar!" and "Lies!" The judge sternly reprimanded her, saying, "If you can't control yourself, I am going to put a muzzle on you." I cringed with embarrassment. By scolding my client like that, I felt like the judge was scolding me, too, by extension.

I've been called a lot of vicious names by adversaries and even by clients (fortunately, not very often, but occasionally it happens). Lawyers are an easy target for people to lash out on. The unfortunate fact is that, typically, you don't hire a lawyer unless you're already in a very difficult position. When clients hire me, they're not always at their best. Emotions run hot. Fears and accusations come tumbling out—often without any basis in reality.

How do I manage this type of negativity?

Mainly, because I've come to accept that it's just part of the job.

If you're a doctor, your job is to welcome sick people into your clinic and help them feel better.

If you're a lawyer, your job is to welcome angry, hurt, frightened, desperate, and sometimes oppressed people into your office and help them feel better—and also, to seek the best and fairest possible outcome for their situation.

When I feel attacked or criticized, I find that the best thing to do is listen. I try not to react or respond right away. Just listen.

Even if my client is crying, shouting, enraged, or saying things that are patently untrue, my job is to listen patiently until my client has expressed whatever he or she needs to say. Interrupting is not helpful—that usually makes my client feel like I'm "not hearing" them, making them feel even worse than they already do.

Even if my client's outburst feels unfair or untrue, it's still worth listening to, because that outburst is a perspective—a point of view—that I need to understand in order to do my job well.

Abraham Lincoln—who was a lawyer before he was elected President of the United States—once said, *"Whatever you are, be a good one."*

Part of being a good lawyer means listening calmly and respectfully—to a client, to a judge, to your opponent in court—even when it is not easy to do so.

The same could be said for almost any profession. When you feel criticized, your knee-jerk reaction might be to exclaim "That's unfair!" or "Not true!" or "Lies!" or to try to explain or justify your behavior. Instead, say nothing at first. Instead of focusing on how to defend yourself, focus on understanding the other person's perspective. Where is this anger coming from? What's really going on here? Is there a kernel of truth embedded in this outburst? What information can you glean from what he or she is saying? What does this person really need in this moment? Comfort? Reassurance? A new course of action? A meal? Some time to rest or take a break?

Stephen R. Covey once wrote, *"Most people do not listen with the intent to understand; they listen with the intent to reply."*

Try to listen with the intent to understand. Very few people actually do this.

If you do, you'll stand out in your profession and quickly earn people's respect.

* * *

SURVIVAL TIP:

You can't control the people around you, but you're always in control of your own mind, and your own mouth and fingers. Think carefully before you blurt out—or email, text, or post—something you might later regret.

If you can train yourself to handle stressful situations with composure, then—as this attorney points out—you'll always stand out in your industry and win people's respect.

Plus, you'll feel proud of yourself for handling things like a pro—instead of having a face-palm, *"Why did I **say** that?"* moment tomorrow morning.

I'VE BEEN WAITING FOR AN HOUR!

It was a deliriously beautiful Saturday morning in Portland—the kind of morning that Pacific Northwesterners wait, hope, and pray for all winter long.

The cherry blossom trees were in full bloom, and luscious pink and white blossoms fluttered through the air like birthday confetti. The sky was the prettiest shade of robin's egg blue. It was warm enough to get away with nothing aside from a T-shirt, no jacket required. This weekend couldn't possibly get any better, but then it did—Brandon and I found out that HunnyMilk, the brunch restaurant we started together, had just received a hugely positive review in the local newspaper. *Score!*

"It's going to be a great weekend," I told Brandon, giving him a big squeeze. I knew this review would bring tons of curious new customers into our restaurant. And I was right.

At 9:00 a.m., when we opened our doors, there was already a line of thirty people waiting outside. That had *never* happened before. I felt a combination of joy, gratitude, excitement...and sinking dread. We were just a baby restaurant—only a couple months old—and we had a tiny dining room with limited seating, not to mention limited staff. Back in those days, the whole team was just me, Brandon, and Brandon's buddy Donnie. Brandon and Donnie handled the cooking. I was in charge of... everything else.

If you've ever been an all-in-one hostess/waitress/ manager, you know that handling a packed restaurant

filled with thirty hungry brunch customers is no
easy feat.

I had to seat everyone, take everyone's orders, attempt to
stagger the orders so that Brandon and Donnie wouldn't
be inundated with too many meals at once, make all
the coffee drinks and brunch cocktails, field questions
("Is the bacon organic? Don't you have any gluten-free
waffles?"), refill water pitchers, and get on my hands and
knees to clean up biscuit crumbs and spilled Cheerios off
the floor—because the stroller-moms and their infants
always leave an endless trail of Cheerio dust in their
wake. It was like a game of Brunch Tetris, with many
moving pieces that I had to single-handedly maneuver to
keep everyone happy.

In between doing all of that, I had to sprint into the
kitchen to wash piles of dishes by hand (we didn't have
a dishwasher on our team at that point) so that Brandon
and Donnie actually had clean plates to serve meals on.
My heart was pounding. My stress levels were tipping
into the danger zone. I felt like an air traffic controller,
trying to coordinate thirty different incoming flights. It
was bonkers.

Meanwhile, customers kept arriving. Our tiny waiting
area became packed to the gills, and people started lining
up outside. The line curled around the block. It was our
dream come true—tons of customers, hooray!—except
in that moment, it felt more like a nightmare. My brain
was completely overloaded. Every step I took, someone
needed something from me:

"Got any hot sauce?"

"Could I get a refill on this?"

"Mine was supposed to come with avocado."

"How long till our food comes?"

"How long till we can get a table?"

"Hey, the bathroom's out of toilet paper."

"Can I get change for a twenty?"

"Oops, I spilled something. Sorry."

"Oops, I spilled something again. Could you get that?"

Somehow, through the grace of the Brunch Gods, I managed to keep everything running relatively smoothly. I smiled cheerily and used my best "soothing yoga-goddess voice" with every customer. I projected an air of total ease and control. But inside? I was one biscuit crumb away from a nervous breakdown.

At 1:00 p.m., I could see the light at the end of the tunnel. We closed the kitchen at 2:00 p.m., so I just had to survive one more hour of this mayhem. Problem was, we still had a massive line of customers waiting for a table. Some had been waiting forty, fifty, sixty minutes or more. Several people sighed, grumbled, and trudged away in defeat because they were tired of waiting so long.

Every time I glanced towards the waiting area, I saw "hangry" (hungry + angry) facial expressions, glazed eyes, and disappointment. These people wanted to sit and eat *now*. But there was nothing I could do to make things move along faster.

Every time a table opened up, I'd dash over and call out the next person's name on the list. I tried to seat everyone as rapidly as humanly possible.

"Kevin, party of two!" "Dalia, party of five!"

I called out one woman's name—let's call her "Rita"—but nobody responded.

"Rita? Rita? Party of two?" I called out again. No one stirred. I figured she must have been one of the customers who trudged away to find brunch somewhere else. I called her name one last time, and then crossed her name off the list. "I guess she's gone."

I dove back into the frenzied dining room, where dozens of new customers needed coffee and mimosas ASAP. Ten to twenty minutes later, I felt a tap on my shoulder.

"*Why* is my name crossed off the list?" a woman asked me, with rage blazing in her eyes. She pointed at the wait-list where I'd crossed off the name "Rita."

Uh-oh. Return of the Rita.

"We've been waiting for over an *hour*," she added, with a tone that sounded more like she was saying, "We've been starving in the cruel streets without shelter for *ten years*!"

I did exactly what you're supposed to do. I apologized for the long wait. I explained that I'd called out her name several times, but that nobody had responded. I explained that I'd assumed, mistakenly, that she had left. I apologized again for the misunderstanding.

She looked at me with absolute disgust, as if I was the stupidest person she'd ever encountered.

"My friend and I were standing right outside," she told me. "Why didn't you call my name *outside*? I was *right there*."

I tried to sort through the memories in my scrambled egg brain. Didn't I call her name outside, as well as inside? I thought I did. But maybe I didn't. It's entirely possible that I forgot to do that.

I apologized again, profusely, and told her I'd seat her at the next available table.

"It will probably be just fifteen more minutes..."

"*Oh, come on!* This is *ridiculous!*"

Now Rita wasn't just irritated—she was yelling at me. Actual yelling. Full volume.

The waiting area went silent.

Several customers set down their smartphones, stopped texting and Instagramming and Snapchatting, and turned their attention towards the dramatic scene that was unfolding.

Everyone stared at me with stunned, pitying glances— and right then, something snapped inside of me. There was something about Rita's tone that felt so mean, so insulting, as if she thought I was "a dumb, incompetent waitress," some type of "lesser being" who didn't even deserve basic human courtesy.

I could feel tears welling up in my eyes, and I knew I wouldn't be able to hold them back much longer. I mumbled one final apology to Rita and then dashed into the kitchen, where my pent-up tears could finally gush out. I sobbed into the sink, which was piled high with grimy dishes.

Brandon rushed over to see what was wrong. I recapped what had happened, and then grabbed his forearm.

"I need you with me," I told him. "Please come. Right now."

I didn't want to face Rita again by myself.

I dragged a very bewildered Brandon out to the waiting area, found Rita, took a deep breath, and then said:

"Hi again, Rita. I'm Alex. This is Brandon. And this our restaurant. We run this place together. I wanted to apologize again for the mix-up with the waiting list. And again, I am sorry that you've had to wait so long for a table. We'll be able to seat you any minute now. And Brandon and I would like to give you and your friend both of your meals on the house. No charge."

I honestly don't know how I did it, but I made my little speech with a completely calm tone of voice. I was trembling slightly, and I was squeezing Brandon's arm with an iron grip, but I managed to smile and speak kindly to Rita and her friend. And I made sure to speak loudly enough so that everyone in the waiting area could hear me, because I wanted everyone to know, "This is how we handle 'problems' at HunnyMilk, and this is how we communicate to each other."

Instantly, Rita's sour expression melted away. She actually looked slightly embarrassed, as if she'd just realized how awful she was being. I can't know for sure, of course, but I suspect that when I explained that Brandon and I were the owners of the restaurant, it was a "wake-up" moment for Rita. Maybe she realized that we aren't just faceless, nameless brunch drones. We're actual people. We're the people who created this entire place. We have dreams, goals, and feelings. We're *human beings*.

"Uh, OK, that sounds great," she mumbled in response. I walked away and Brandon followed.

Back in the kitchen, he told me, "I am so sorry you had to deal with her. Next time, just come get me, and I'll deal with it."

"It's fine," I told him. And I meant it. My sob-fest was over. I felt strong and proud. I marched back into the dining room and knocked out the last thirty minutes of service with my head held high.

When Rita and her friend finished their meals, they tried to pay, but I insisted: "Nope, everything's on the house. I insist." They accepted, and Rita gave me a weak smile and said, "Well, thank you very much." She left. I exhaled with relief, feeling my shoulders un-clench as she passed through the exit.

After closing up for the day, Brandon and I rushed home and flopped face-down on our bed. Our muscles ached. Our feet were throbbing. My hands were waterlogged and wrinkly, and my nail polish had completely peeled off after hours of dish-washing.

"Holy...whoa," I said. Brandon nodded. "That was intense."

And then, we did what entrepreneurs do. We got a clipboard, and some paper, and we started problem-solving.

Problem: We're getting a lot busier and we have more customers than ever before. (It's a "good" problem to have, but...it's still a problem.)

Solution: We need to hire a few people to expand our staff. One host/server for the entire restaurant is not enough anymore.

OK, that first problem was fairly easy to solve. But we had a second problem, which was a little more interesting.

Problem: People *hate* waiting for a table, especially when they're already hungry. They get grumpy and impatient. It creates an obnoxious atmosphere for everyone in the entire restaurant.

Solution: What could we do? Brandon and I started brainstorming. We could send out little snacks to tide them over until it's time for their actual meal. Little bite-sized nibbles of coffee cake. Mini pancakes with blueberry jam. Things like that. And also, hmm, could we entertain them, somehow, so that waiting isn't so boring?

"We could put some board games and books in the waiting area," I suggested.

"And coloring sheets and Crayons. And Nintendo!" Brandon added.

"What about some card games? And a chess board?"

Yes! Nobody else in town had a super-fun waiting area like this. This would be original and noteworthy. People would totally love it.

"Let's make our waiting area so fun that people actually feel sad when it's time to get a table, sit down, and order their meal," I told Brandon.

That's what we did. That week, we ordered tons of games and supplies on Amazon. Brandon found an old Nintendo set on eBay that was incredibly cheap. I painted a huge sign to let customers know about our new-and-improved waiting area. We placed this sign at the front of the restaurant where everybody could see it. It was a huge hit.

Just as we suspected, people *loved* the game-filled waiting area.

"OMG, you guys have *Nintendo*!" people would exclaim. "And *Twister*? This is the best." Instead of staring at their phones and sighing with boredom, customers started writing letters, coloring, playing games, laughing, and interacting with each other. The vibe in the room went from "hangry" to "neighborly and happy."

Our new waiting area led to some additional media attention, too. A couple of new reviews came out online—and in a few other local papers and magazines—talking about our delicious food and our creative, whimsical waiting area.

Best of all? I never got screamed at by Rita—or anybody else—ever again.

As strange as it may sound, I'm glad that Rita exploded and yelled at me, because her brunch-rage inspired me and Brandon to upgrade certain aspects of the restaurant that weren't working. Because of Rita, we wrote down specific customer service policies, tightened up our systems, hired more staff members, and made all kinds of positive improvements to prevent "Rita Episodes" from happening again in the future. Our restaurant is even more popular and successful today, thanks in part to Rita's outburst.

So thanks, Rita. Wherever you are today, I hope you're being seated promptly, and I hope you're well-fed and happy. I wish you the best.

When a customer, client, or boss is completely furious with you, refuses to pay you, or starts screaming at you in front of a crowd of people, it can feel like the worst moment of your entire life. You want to sink into a crack in the floor and disappear from existence. But afterwards, once you're safely back at home, you've got a big opportunity. Now you get to use your savvy, creative brain to come up with a solution. Because every problem has a solution. And whatever solution you come up with…it might catapult your entire career, or business into the next level of success.

***

SURVIVAL TIP:

When you feel attacked or criticized by your boss (or by a client or customer), ask yourself, *"What's the problem here that needs to be solved?"*

Try not to take their irritation personally. In all likelihood, they're probably not upset with you, personally. They're upset with "the situation" and they're lashing out in frustration—possibly, in a really unprofessional way.

But you don't have to sink to that level. You can take the high road. You can stay cool and professional. You can make it your personal mission to solve the problem in a creative, inspiring way—and you'll be everyone's hero when you do.

Chapter Four:

When Bullies and Internet Goblins Are Ruining Your Life

SPEWING RAINBOWS

I couldn't believe what I was hearing.

"There's a website where people do...what?"

I was having lunch with my friend Sarah, and she was in the midst of telling me a strange, depressing story about one of the murkiest corners of the Internet.

As Sarah explained to me, there's a special website where people gather to gossip and write snarky things about popular bloggers. Sort of like a virtual water cooler where the topic of conversation is: "Which blogger is the ugliest and stupidest? Who has the worst hair? Whose e-book is totally lame? Who's getting fat? Who just got divorced—LOL! Let's discuss!"

I didn't get it.

"Uh, so...why does this website exist? What's the point? It just sounds so mean."

Sarah shrugged. No idea. Maybe these people think it's fun to rip apart certain bloggers, especially once they get a little "too famous." Maybe they feel it's an important type of discussion to have, for whatever reason. Maybe they get some type of cathartic release by writing vicious things about other people, especially from behind the safety blanket of Internet anonymity. Maybe it's a power trip, like bullying someone at school.

"Have they ever written about you on that website?" I asked Sarah. She runs a popular travel and lifestyle blog with thousands of readers.

"Not very often, thank God," she replied. "But they write about Sally all the time."

This stunned me. Sally, our mutual friend, is one of the kindest, loveliest human beings I've ever known. She's a personal stylist, and she's passionate about helping her clients to fall in love with their bodies, regardless of their size, and express themselves through clothing and accessories.

She's warm, generous, and she genuinely loves helping women to feel better about themselves. She's the type of person who says, "Instead of bringing me a birthday gift this year, please read a poem or perform a special talent!"

In short: Sally is an absolute delight.

I couldn't imagine anyone saying anything bad about her. It would be like someone saying nasty things about Santa Claus or Ellen DeGeneres or Michelle Obama. Unthinkable.

I needed to see this for myself.

One night, I popped over to the gossip website that Sarah had told me about. It felt like submerging myself in a pool of sticky, noxious tar. Seriously unsettling.

Within just a few minutes, I found postings filled with hateful comments about dozens of bloggers—many of whom were my personal friends and colleagues.

"Absurd"

"Boring"

"Dumb"

"Fake"

"Frumpy"

"Fugly"

"Gross"

"Horse-facey"

"Losers"

"Self-absorbed"

"A closeted chunkster"

"A histrionic bitch"

"The kind of girl who'll have a baby to increase page views"

The vicious jabs went on and on and on. Some of the conversation threads were hundreds of pages long. The website users mocked bloggers' clothes, hair, weight and bodies. They mocked bloggers' ideas, creative projects, philanthropic initiatives, and religious beliefs. They even made sport of their relationships, pregnancies, and children.

One particularly charming post simply ended with:

"Whatever. I hate her."

I read numerous posts about Sally, and other wonderful people that I know, and my heart started pounding. I felt a surge of adrenaline. My feet tapped the floor anxiously. I was upset. More than that—I was angry.

"This is not OK," I thought to myself.

And then, I sat down and started to write.

I wrote an essay about gossiping and bullying, and why it's unacceptable to treat each other this way. I wrote about Tricia Norman—the mother of a teenage girl who committed suicide after being terrorized by bullies. I urged people to think carefully about how the words you post onto the Internet can impact people's lives.

My main point was, if you want to spend your precious time posting something online, post something that will make the world kinder, safer, better, and more beautiful—not uglier.

I ended my essay with these words:

"The world needs your best, not your worst. Your help, not your hate. Your strength, not your snark."

The essay poured out of me rapidly and fiercely, like a torrential downpour. I emailed it to my newsletter subscribers. Within hours, my inbox was flooded with responses from people all over the world:

"Thank you for saying this, and for taking a stand..."

"I've been dealing with a lot of nasty criticism from this same particular online forum. In fact, I'm the pregnant one whose unborn child they're mocking—along with my ideas, creativity, what I look like, and the things I write. Thank you for having my back..."

"Knowing that there are people like you out there, makes it easier for me to overcome my fears of those other types of people out there..."

It's always great to know that your words are having an effect on people. I felt proud of myself for taking a stance on a difficult topic. That felt good.

But then, of course...the bullies came after me.

While I hadn't mentioned their virtual watering hole by name, the bullies knew I was talking about them. Word travels fast on the Internet. Within hours, a new conversation thread started up on the site, and this time, it wasn't about Sally or Sarah or any of my other friends and colleagues. It was all about *me*—how stupid I was, how I didn't understand their perspective, how my writing was terrible, and how I was annoying, idiotic, and...you get the idea.

It felt nightmarish to read all of these comments about me and the piece I'd written. I was trying to encourage people to communicate with more compassion—in return, I get flame-broiled on the exact site I'd been writing about.

Then, I had an idea:

"I'll have a conversation with these people and try to understand their perspective," I thought to myself. "Maybe I'll be able to persuade them to behave differently—to stop writing awful, snarky things as a form of daily entertainment. Maybe I can change their minds and hearts. Maybe that's possible. Anything's possible, right?"

I created a new account so that I could participate on the website and respond to the things that were being said about me. I wanted to be part of the conversation. I wanted to speak to these forum posters directly, and let them know, "Actually, I'm not closed off to your perspective. Personally, I think what you're doing here on this website is cruel, hurtful, and really unproductive, but many of you disagree strongly. So, tell me more. I'm open to hearing your side of things."

I'm sorry to report: it didn't work.

Nobody was interested in having a dialogue with me, and the conversation thread grew increasingly vitriolic.

One poster encouraged me to *"Go spew your Mister Rogers rainbows"* somewhere else. (That was probably one of the "nicer" suggestions directed towards me on that site.)

After a few stressful, stomach-twisting days, I realized: *"I'm not getting anywhere. I need to step away."*

I posted one last note in the forum, logged off, and never went back.

Sometimes, when you're pummeling yourself against an immovable boulder, getting absolutely nowhere, the only sane thing to do is...back away.

The Internet is full of bright pockets as well as dark, poisonous corners. I might be naive, but I still believe there's more brightness out there than darkness.

On the Internet, and everywhere else in life, you'll find what my hero Fred Rogers called *"the helpers"*—people who are driven to help, to serve, to bring positivity and hope into the world.

"When I was a boy and I would see scary things in the news, my mother would say to me, 'Look for the helpers.' You will always find people who are helping," Fred once said.

When I see scary things in the news, or vicious things happening online, I think about Fred's words. I think about the helpers—and I strive to be one of them.

OK, maybe I wasn't able to convince thousands of people in that online forum to change, or see things differently, or stop writing cruel things about people just for entertainment. Still, making the effort was worth it. Even if you don't succeed in your mission, I believe that trying is always worth it.

If nothing else, I know—based on the deluge of emails that I received—that hundreds of people in my community felt safer just knowing that someone was willing to say, *"Bullying is not OK."*

Sally definitely felt that way. After reading my essay about bullying, she wrote me an email to say:

"As a frequent target, I have struggled to find a way to respond or react that wouldn't result in making my situation worse. Thank you for being brave and taking a stand and saying what should be incredibly obvious to anyone with two brain cells and a beating heart."

When you take a stand for something you believe in, there's bound to be some blowback. You might get the occasional piece of hate mail. You might get mocked or shamed. You might have certain readers who misunderstand you, or who take your words out of context and twist them into nonsensical sound bites. You might have to endure all of that, and more.

But then, in the midst of all that, you might also get an email from someone like Sally, saying, "Thank you for being brave." Or an email from a teenager halfway around the world saying, "I was having an awful day, but then I read your latest blog post, and now I feel better."

You might get an email like that. And then you know...all the stress, all the vulnerability, all the discouragement...

It's all worth it.

* * *

SURVIVAL TIP:

When the trolls, bullies, and insensitive critics of the world are getting you down, think about all of the reasons why you're doing your work.

Think about the people who feel better, happier, and stronger because of what you're doing. Think about your fans—even if you only have three fans right now. Think about the positive ripple that you're creating in the world. Focus on *that*.

If you're one of *"the helpers,"* then you can take deep pride in that. Know that—somewhere, out there—someone really appreciates everything that you're doing. It might not always seem like it, but people are watching you, and people are influenced by what you write, say, post, and do. You might be helping more people than you even realize, just by being brave, and just by being you.

ARROGANT. YUCKY. I CAN'T DO IT.

On April 5, 2013 at 9:23 a.m., I received the following email from a woman named "Alice." (Name changed for her privacy.)

The backstory:

Alice signed up to receive my weekly e-newsletter. After a few months, she decided she wanted to unsubscribe. When you unsubscribe, you have the option to tick various boxes to explain why you are unsubscribing. You also have the option to type in a personal reason for why you no longer wish to hear from me.

This was Alice's reason:

I really loved what I was reading at first, but over the last few months I've felt Alexandra has gotten really arrogant. It's great that she's becoming successful but she doesn't have any humility, thinks she's the greatest thing ever and I find it really uncomfortable and yucky to read. Reading your stuff no longer makes me feel good. Can't do it anymore.

This happened years ago, but I still remember it vividly. I remember reading Alice's note over and over, feeling sick to my stomach, hurt, and confused. Specific words and phrases kept echoing inside my mind: "Arrogant." "Doesn't have any humility." "Yucky." "Can't do it."

I remember thinking, *"I don't think those statements are true. I don't think I'm that type of person."* But of course, I also couldn't help but wonder, *"Or what if she's right?"*

My boyfriend urged me to ignore the message. Don't respond. Just let it go.

But I couldn't let it go. I decided to reply. I wrote a personal note to Alice.

My note said:

It sounds like my writing isn't resonating with you anymore. I'm sorry to hear that.

It's interesting to hear that you feel I've become "arrogant" and devoid of "humility." I doubt that you intended for those words to feel hurtful, but they did.

While it's true that I've enjoyed some success in recent years, my goal is always to make my readers feel inspired, empowered, and capable of enjoying their own version of success. And while I'm certainly not perfect, I try to pass along everything I'm learning along the way.

I can see how my positive, upbeat tone might come across as arrogant—but that's certainly not my intention.

I never expected to hear anything further from Alice.

She surprised me.

She wrote:

I appreciate you taking the time to write to me. I think you are very talented, have a lot of great advice to offer, and I'm sorry you were hurt by what I said. I didn't mean for it to come across so harshly, so I apologize for the caustic tone that was on my part unintentional.

A few minutes later, she sent another follow-up reply:

Hi Alex. I'm feeling really bad and embarrassed now, I really didn't mean to hurt you and I think was also a bit vulnerable this morning and perhaps unfairly projecting things onto you. I sincerely apologize.

I responded:

No need to feel embarrassed. I'm glad we could have this dialogue—and I hope that whatever's making you feel a bit vulnerable gets resolved.

P.S. I just peeked at your blog. As someone who has also recovered from an eating disorder, I want to say: you're doing beautiful, important work. Keep it up.

Our email exchange continued—back and forth—and ultimately ended on a very positive, mutually respectful note. (I was very surprised by the outcome. It was unexpected and beautiful.)

I learned a lot from my conversation with Alice. The lessons still ripple through my life today.

I learned that you might have the best of intentions (to help, teach, inspire, uplift), but somewhere out there, someone might feel like your tone is arrogant (or stupid, bossy, mean, greedy, too bubbly, too boring, what have you). There is not much you can do to change this. You can control how you write, but you can't always control how your writing is absorbed and perceived by others. This is the reality of being a writer (or engaging in any other art form). It's something that must be accepted.

Sometimes, people have bad days, and they do unintentionally cruel things. You do it. I do it, too. We all do. No one is perfect in this regard.

Sometimes, people see a blank Internet form ("Enter your comments here") and use that form as a therapeutic venting-box—forgetting that eventually, those words are going to reach an actual, living human being with actual human feelings.

Sometimes—not always, but sometimes—it is possible to have a civil, respectful, and humane conversation with someone who has criticized you harshly, who sees the world very differently than you, or even someone who deeply dislikes you. This gives me great hope for humanity, particularly in our current political climate.

The next time you feel sharply criticized—by a stranger on the Internet, by your boss, your client, perhaps your own parent, child, or partner—I hope this story about me and Alice brings some comfort to you.

I hope this story reminds you that what people say about you isn't always true, that people say things for all kinds of reasons (some of which involve you, some of which do not), and that even if harsh words have been exchanged, it is still possible to talk further, to understand one another a bit better, and potentially to reach a positive conclusion.

Minds can change, hearts can open, surprising connections can form, apologies can be shared, wounds can be healed—sometimes in the span of just a few hours (or emails).

Miracles like this happen every day.

* * *

SURVIVAL TIP:

Sometimes, when you feel attacked by someone on the Internet, there's no point in trying to start a conversation with that person. Often, they're simply not interested— or they've firmly made up their mind about you, and they're unwilling to budge an inch. You're just going to be banging your head against a brick wall.

But other times, that's not the case. Not often, but once in a while, there's a way to have a calm, reasonable—even uplifting—conversation with someone who previously didn't "like" you or "get" you. Even someone who has said something really mean about you.

That happened for me, as you read in this last story. So, keep a little spark of optimism burning in your heart. Try, if you want, to reach out and bridge the divide. You never know what could happen next.

Sometimes, bullies can see the error of their ways. Sometimes, rude mailing list subscribers can apologize, retract their comments, or even want to become your friend. People can be very mean and careless. But people can also be very surprising. Nothing is permanently etched in stone. Hearts can shift. Minds can open. People can change.

SCAM ARTIST!

Story contributed by: Melissa Cassera.
Entrepreneur. Business consultant. TV screenwriter.

A Note from Alexandra:

Let's see...what can I tell you about Melissa? Where to begin?

Melissa runs a consulting company where she helps people start cool, creative businesses, find clients, and make a living doing what they love. She's also a former actress and model who once appeared on the cover of a nursing industry magazine posing as a "sad uterine fibroids patient." (Oh, the glamour!) On top of all that, she's also a screenwriter, and she recently sold her first original series to a TV network. It's a show that exposes the scandalous behind-the-scenes drama that happens in the pharmaceutical sales industry. (I literally can't wait to watch it when it comes out. I've already pre-stocked my cupboard with popcorn.)

Melissa is a modern-day Renaissance Woman. She has figured out how to juggle numerous passions and creative projects while also making time for her husband Gary, her friends like me, and her clan of furry dog-babies. And somehow, she's never too busy to email me the latest *Fifty Shades* movie teaser. Which I always appreciate.

What I love most about Melissa is that she believes, in the core of her being, that life is supposed to be *fun*. As she frequently reminds me: *"Going to work should feel like a guilty pleasure."*

But even when you've created your dream career, that doesn't mean every single day is a cakewalk. Once in a while, you're bound to encounter a colleague, customer, or client who is...uh, shall we say, "emotionally unhinged."

Maybe it's someone who overreacts wildly over the smallest little thing. Or maybe it's someone who makes unfair assumptions about you, or gossips about you behind your back. Or maybe it's someone who leaps onto the Internet and posts disparaging comments about you, dragging your name through the mud, creating a PR nightmare—not to mention, a broken heart.

This is the story of how Melissa dealt with her first PR disaster in a remarkably positive way. It wasn't exactly a "pleasurable" experience for Melissa. Nonetheless, as you'll see, she handled it with class.

* * *

Melissa: A few years ago, both my grandpop and best friend died of cancer—one day apart.

It sounds unreal, but it actually happened.

It was a heart-wrenching time. My stomach felt like it was full of acid. I could barely eat or sleep. Everyone in my life and community was incredibly kind and supportive—except one person.

This particular person was interested in hiring me for marketing and business coaching. She found my website, paid the fee for an hour of coaching, and then emailed me multiple times, eager to set up her first appointment. At least, that's what she claims. (The reality is: I never received a single email from her. I checked my inbox. I checked my spam box. I checked my trash folder. Nothing. But back to that in a moment...)

Long story short: after (supposedly) emailing me multiple times and hearing nothing in response, this person got *pissed*. She decided that I was some kind of "scam artist," stealing people's money with wild abandon! She logged into a very popular online forum for business owners and wrote a scathing post about me and how I had "ripped her off."

Meanwhile, I'm grieving two deaths and barely keeping myself together. I didn't know about this forum post for several days—and during that time, nearly one hundred comments were posted from people who didn't know me, commiserating with the angry woman who felt ripped off, and basically hoping I'd rot in hell.

Fortunately, a close friend noticed the scathing post, added her own comment to defend my honor, and then alerted me about it.

I assessed the situation and decided to contact the upset woman directly. I politely explained that I'd never received any emails from her, and could she possibly resend or forward the emails that, somehow, had gotten lost in the shuffle? She refused to resend them (or couldn't, or wouldn't, or whatever).

To this day, I have no idea what actually happened. Maybe this woman did email me, and somehow her emails never came through. That's possible. Or maybe she never actually emailed me, but thought she had, got angry, and then by the time she realized her mistake, had already bad-mouthed me publicly on the Internet and felt too ashamed to admit that maybe she had made an error (and that maybe she had *slightly* overreacted). That's possible, too.

In the end, I decided to take the high road. I went into the forum and posted a brief note explaining that communication breakdowns happen sometimes, and it's always frustrating, but very fixable. I responded from a calm, professional state of mind.

My classy response earned me a lot of fans. Several forum users posted notes saying that I had handled the situation with grace, and perhaps the original poster shouldn't have jumped to the conclusion that I was scamming her. That person simply wrote: "I know my truth" and then left the discussion. I finally shut everything off, had a good cry, and then took the rest of the night away from the Internet.

That wasn't the only time I've ever been criticized in a public forum—but that was definitely one of the worst, especially since everything was compounded by grief and loss.

What I've learned is that when you feel criticized or bullied, you always have options. You can walk away. You can engage. You can defend your honor. You can take the high road. You can try to control the situation before it blows completely out of control. Every situation is unique, but generally, if you maintain a calm and classy tone, people will see that you're not a monster, and most (sane) people will see your humanity, forgive you (if forgiveness is even necessary!), and quickly move on.

I've also learned that one piece of public criticism—no matter how vicious—is not going to wreck your career. If you've built a strong, positive reputation, one nasty review is not going to tear your empire apart.

And lastly, I've learned that when someone tramples across your business (or life) spewing all kinds of rage-filled negativity, it's usually because something is screwed up in their world—not yours.

For example, if you own a restaurant and a customer shows up in a sour mood, maybe it's because they had a fight with their spouse. And now they're not hungry. And now you're shoving your menu and cheery attitude into their sad world, and that might be a sucky experience for them. So they gripe on Yelp about your awful restaurant, and honestly, it has nothing to do with you. That's hard to accept as an artist or business owner—but it's the truth. And there's not really much you can do to change their opinion about you. That's hard to accept, too.

To this day, the missing-email-person probably thinks I'm a scammy, horrible human being. I can't change that. Something made her believe she was doing the right thing by writing a post to "warn" other people about my horribleness. I can't change that either. The only thing I can do is not take it personally, and just let it go.

If you feel criticized, whether fairly or unfairly, try to change what you can—and accept what you can't. In my experience, that's the healthiest approach, and one that will keep you sane.

* * *

SURVIVAL TIP:

If someone is blathering all over the Internet, talking about what a terrible person (or business owner) you are, you might need to step up and become your own Public Relations Director. Just like Olivia Pope from *Scandal*, you need to become a "Fixer" and smooth out the crisis, as best you can. Your reputation may depend on it.

Happily, as we learned from Melissa's story, if you respond to the crisis with grace and professionalism, you can quickly turn a negative situation into a positive moment that *enhances* your credibility rather than ruining it.

People will notice how calm and unflustered you're being, and how elegantly you're handling the situation, and they'll respect you for that. Channel your inner Michelle Obama, Dalai Lama—or the calm, measured hero of your choice—and set the record straight. As Melissa notes, your classy response will earn you a lot of new fans.

MEAN NEIGHBOR LADY.

Story contributed by: Shelley Cohen.
Creative director. Life, style, and confidence coach for women.

Note from Alexandra:

My friend Melissa—whom you met in the previous story—introduced me to Shelley via email.

"You've got to interview Shelley for your book," Melissa told me. "She's got a story that will make you cringe."

Melissa was right. This story is highly cringe-inducing. It's one of those stories that makes you think, "I can't believe how *awful* some people can be!"

Yup. Some people are seriously just...wow. Unbelievable. It's like they went to the University of Assholery and majored in "Publicly Shaming People And Mocking Their Dreams" with a minor in "Being A Complete Dick Because Hey, Why Not?"

Shelley had the unfortunate experience of meeting a U of A graduate, and this is what happened...

* * *

Shelley: Not long ago, my husband I moved to a new town where I didn't know many people.

One afternoon, my super-sweet next-door neighbor asked if I'd like to pop over for a social drink. She mentioned that some other peeps from around the neighborhood would be there, and it would be a great opportunity for me to meet a few of them. My hubby was out of town, and I had no plans that evening, so I thought, *"Why not?"*

I went over to join the party and grabbed a glass of wine.

After chatting with some lovely people for about twenty minutes, the conversations dispersed, and I found myself momentarily standing there, alone, with my half-empty glass of wine. Right at that moment, a lady I'd never seen or met before approached me and loudly asked, "Where are your people?"

Slightly taken aback by the question, I responded, "My 'person' is out of town on business, and the rest of my people are back in Houston and Australia." I explained that I was new to Louisiana because my husband was recently relocated for work.

After the lady asked what my husband does for work, she said, "Well, what do you do?"

Right away, based on this woman's tone and demeanor, I had a sinking feeling that she wasn't going to understand—or approve of—the type of work I do. But I went ahead and explained anyway.

I said something along these lines:

"I'm a life, style and confidence coach for women. I help my clients to discover and express their personal style, develop a personal brand, and build tons of confidence to pursue their goals and passions. My work is a hybrid of 'creative direction' and 'styling' and 'life coaching'. In a nutshell, I guess you could say I'm kinda like a 'personal stylist' with some added extras."

For a few seconds, there was silence...and then... hysterical, loud laughter.

"Oh my God! Oh my God! Oh my God! Did you hear what she said? Did you hear what she said?" The lady began tapping people on the shoulder and elbowing those close to her to get their attention. One by one, everyone at the party (about fourteen people in total) stopped their conversations and turned to see what was going on. All eyes on me.

The lady said, "Repeat what you just told me." So I did.

Once again, the lady broke into hysterical laughter and said to everyone, "Isn't that the most stupid thing you've ever heard in your life?"

That is the actual word she used:

Stupid.

I almost couldn't believe it. Was I being punked? Surely this wasn't real. I felt so humiliated. I wanted the ground to open and swallow me whole.

Everyone in the room looked equally embarrassed. A few people shot me sympathetic glances, a few nodded in semi-agreement with the mean lady, and most just awkwardly shuffled away and resumed their earlier conversations.

But the mean lady wasn't done with me yet...

Next, she said to me, "Well, I bet you don't have many clients!"

I replied, "Actually, the opposite is true. Because my business is completely location-independent, I have clients in Germany, the UK, LA, Houston, New York, Canada, Australia. All over the world. And I can work from anywhere in the world!"

The mean lady's face changed. She looked shocked, as if she'd just been tasered. She walked closer to me and said, "You know what? I just want to shake your clients because they are *so* stupid for paying you anything!"

Before walking away, the mean lady threw in one last jab:

"I see things in black and white. I'm an accountant. Now *that's* a real job!"

She sauntered off, evidently pleased with herself, and I was left standing alone thinking, "Did that seriously just happen?"

If the "mean lady incident" had happened twelve months earlier, I probably would have completely fallen apart. I probably would have run home, bawled my eyes out, and rapidly inhaled an entire sleeve of Oreo cookies. After that, I probably would have stared at my business website, obsessively worrying about every single sentence on every page, overanalyzing every detail and wondering, *"Is she right? Am I stupid? Is my profession some kind of joke?"*

Happily, in this instance, I didn't do any of those things.

Yes, I did excuse myself from the party—after saying goodbye to a few (non-insane) neighbors. Yes, I did feel rattled and hurt. But rather than let the mean lady's opinions get under my skin, I took a leaf out of Taylor Swift's songbook: I shook it off.

Back at home, after the party, I took some deep breaths and guided myself through a positive visualization. With my eyes closed, resting on my bed, I visualized myself shaking and flicking the mean lady's negative energy off my body. Inside my mind's eye, I imagined myself encircled by a safe, sparkly bubble that repelled the mean lady's icky energy. By the end of that visualization, I felt so much better.

To this day, I have no idea why my "job description" caused the mean lady at the party to react the way she did. Maybe she felt jealous of my fun, creative profession and the freedom I get to enjoy. Maybe she was taught by her parents, from an early age, that anything related to "fashion" or "style" is inherently stupid and frivolous. Maybe she hired a personal stylist once and had a negative experience that soured her perception of the entire industry. Or maybe she's just a plain old bully. Who knows?

What I do know is that *her* opinions do not get to wreck *my* self-esteem.

Here is my advice:

The next time you feel criticized, first, ask yourself:

"Does the person who is criticizing me have a loving and supportive intention?"

Is she trying to help you avoid a costly mistake? Trying to guide you towards a better solution? Or something to that effect? If so, listen to the criticism with an open mind.

However, if the person who is criticizing you does *not* have a loving and supportive intention (aka: mean lady at the party), then don't listen! Shake it out of your system.

To shake things out, do a positive visualization, or if that's not enough, then try something else to reground yourself: soak in a bathtub filled with scented oils and pink sparkles, light a candle, practice meditation and breathing exercises, take a walk, or write about how the experience made you feel—and as you're writing, try to identify the lessons embedded in whatever just happened to you. (That always helps me.)

I hope you never have to experience what I did at the neighborhood party. I hope no one ever laughs at you— or calls you "stupid"—when you explain your profession. I hope no one ever calls you "stupid," period.

But if that ever happens, try to stand tall. Be confident in who you are, in all of your bright and shiny brilliance. Imagine a glittery pink force field (or another color of your choice!) shielding you, surrounding you, and repelling negative energy from your body. (This may sound silly, but I'm telling you: it works.)

Tell yourself, *"I don't know why this person feels such a strong need to criticize my life, and I may never know, but that's not my concern. Her opinions do not get to determine my self-esteem and happiness. Not now—and not ever."*

Force field: activated. Pink glitter: everywhere. Bullies: defeated.

Love always wins.

* * *

SURVIVAL TIP:

You've got to find some way of protecting yourself against the meanies of the world—because unfortunately, they're out there. They're everywhere. One of them might be your next-door neighbor!

Different strategies work for different people. Maybe, like Shelley, you want to visualize a force field surrounding your body, protecting you from negativity.

Or maybe you want to keep a handwritten note from a friend—*"You're so awesome, I love you, don't ever forget it"*—folded up in your wallet so you can read it whenever you need a pep talk.

Or maybe you want to wear a shirt with a slogan that makes you feel stronger, like "YOU CAN'T STOP ME" or "STRAIGHT UP BOSS." (My friend Susan does that. She has a pretty amazing T-shirt collection.)

Or maybe there's something else that works for you—a yoga class, a long walk, a hot shower, a conversation with a supportive friend, dancing to Shakira and Enrique Iglesias, or watching YouTube videos of Pomeranian puppies playing with balls of string. (Those all work for me!)

Try a few things out. See what helps you feel better. Make a mental note. *"Oh, cool, that works for me."* Then the next time a mean neighbor-lady creepy-crawls into your life, you'll be ready.

THE HATE MAIL IS WORTH IT.

Story contributed by: Susan Hyatt.
Author. Entrepreneur. Life coach. Motivational speaker.

A Note from Alexandra:

You met Susan earlier in this book. To jog your memory, she's the incredible woman who survived a violent assault, put the shattered pieces of her heart back together, and eventually poured her passions, skills, and hard-won life lessons into a business—and a book.

Susan is a true survivor—in every sense of the word. We've become close friends over the years, and every interaction with her leaves me feeling wiser and stronger.

One thing Susan always says to me, and to her clients, is:

"Being passive gets you nowhere. If you want to achieve your goals, or change the world, you can't be submissive and quiet. You've got to speak up. You have to make a scene."

Susan doesn't just tell people to make a scene—she leads by example. She's constantly making all kinds of scenes—online, onstage, on TV, everywhere she goes. Over the years, her bold, outspoken personality has earned her lots of fans—and a handful of haters.

One time, after appearing on the local news to talk about the Women's March in Washington DC, her video got so many threatening comments, the TV station decided to take it off their website. Susan contacted them and implored them to put it back. She wanted her message to be seen and heard—even if it ruffled some people's feathers.

Despite receiving hate mail, and even death threats, Susan is not shutting up—or slowing down. She has important messages that she wants to share about feminism and female empowerment, about women's rights, about the dangerous diet industry and how it's designed to keep women feeling ugly and powerless, and many other topics. She's an inspiration to me—and to anyone who feels nervous about taking a stand, or sharing an unpopular opinion.

In this story, Susan explains why getting the occasional piece of hate mail doesn't really matter to her anymore—and why she refuses to stand on the sidelines and be silenced.

* * *

Susan: To run a business, you really need nerves of steel.

You face public scrutiny and financial uncertainty. You've got clients who flake out and miss their appointments. You'll deal with people who sign up for events and then back out at the last moment, citing all kinds of excuses—some real, some fake. You've got plagiarists—people stealing your hard work and passing it off as their own. You're putting your heart and soul out there, every day, and there's never any guarantee that you'll be rewarded in the exact way that you want.

And here's the cherry on top: you might get really mean blog comments, mean Facebook comments, or even hate mail from people who have never even met you.

Seriously. It can be tough out there.

As I look back on the past ten years of my career, it's astonishing how much drama I've been through. I absolutely love running my own business, and I believe I was born to be an entrepreneur, but I gotta tell you...I definitely have moments where I'm like: *"Jesus Christ on a cracker! This is hard!"*

But then, just when my nerves are totally fried, just when I feel like I need a 500-week long vacation, that's usually when I'll get one email, one text message, some little sign from the Universe that reminds me, *"OK. **This** is why I do this."*

I got a message like that recently. It was an email from a thirteen-year-old.

This is what it said:

> *Dear Ms. Susan Hyatt,*
>
> *My mom made me watch your video where you told everyone on Facebook that you are upset about the presidential election. And so is your daughter.*
>
> *I'm so mad too.*
>
> *My mom was worried about me because I am only thirteen and depressed.*

Sometimes I can't get up and go to school. I am transgender and where I live no one believes in that. I feel so lonely and like an outcast.

You told people in your video to go to work to protect the LGBT and other groups that might be in trouble now that Trump was elected.

The video and all those people who commented nice things about it helped me get out of bed today and feel better.

It might have been just a bedtime video to you. But to me it saved my life.

Thank you from Georgia.

When I got that email, I started sobbing.

The funny thing is, just a few hours earlier, I had a client back out of one of my programs and ask for a refund because she didn't like my stance on Trump and the election. And then, right after that, I get this email from a thirteen-year-old saying, *"Thank you for speaking up because your words saved my life."*

When I get an email like that, it makes *everything* worth it.

All the uncertainty, all the hate mail, all the cancelations, all the criticism, all the tough stuff that comes along with running a business...*everything*.

You know what? I am fine with losing the occasional client if it means I can inspire a teenager to stay alive.

If I can help one teenager to see how incredible he or she is, or inspire twenty women to speak up and pursue their dreams, or make any type of positive imprint on the world, then I'm willing to deal with all the challenges that come along with doing this work. I'll take it.

No matter what type of work you do—whether you're a full-time parent, a nine-to-fiver, a teacher, an entrepreneur—there are bright spots in every vocation, and there are challenges. Hang onto the bright spots as best you can.

Remember who you're working for. Remember what you're fighting for. Remember the people who appreciate you and depend on you. Remember the thirteen-year-old kid who looks up to you. Remember all of those people, and don't let the occasional piece of hate mail—or negativity of any kind—bring you down. And don't let *anyone* convince you to be silent, passive, docile, and well-behaved. As the saying goes: *"Well-behaved women seldom make history."*

* * *

SURVIVAL TIP:

The next time you get an encouraging text, email, voicemail, or letter from someone—anyone—hold onto it. Take a screenshot of that text. Print it. Frame it. Put it by your desk. When haters come along, filling your inbox with vile negativity, look at that framed text. Remind yourself, *"For someone out there, my work makes a difference."* Focus on that one person. That thirteen-year-old kid. That student from your class. That client who thinks you're terrific. Keep going. Dedicate the rest of your workday to *them.*

You're Going to Be Judged.

Awhile back, I was teaching a writing class.

Towards the end of the class, someone asked:

"How can I get over my fear of people judging me? I'm nervous to publish my work because I don't want to deal with mean emails, mean blog comments, and things like that. How can I get over this?"

Oof. It's a tough question. Because judgment is everywhere all the time.

"I love his writing." "Her voice annoys me." "Wow, that was completely delicious." "Blech. Too rich for my taste."

We judge people's style, voices, choices, and creative work. We do this instinctively. All day, every day, we have reactions to things. We form opinions about things. We filter things into categories. We judge. We can't help it. It's how human beings operate.

Everyone judges, and everyone gets judged.

One time, I got an email from someone who said: "I love that you include photos of yourself in your newsletter! It's so fun to see the face behind the words."

A few days later, I got an email from another person who said: "I don't like that you put photos into your newsletter. It feels like vanity, and it's diluting your message. I expected more from you. Unsubscribe me."

One time, I got an email from someone who said: "Thank you for being open and transparent about your political beliefs. As a Muslim woman, I feel uneasy and vulnerable right now, and I really appreciated what you said."

Another time, I got an email from another person who said: "I really wish you wouldn't talk about politics. What you said about the election...I just don't think it's right."

It's impossible to please everybody.

What feels "inspiring" to one person might feel like "vanity" to another.

What feels "comforting" to one person might feel "inappropriate" to another.

And on and on it goes.

While it's really frustrating at times, I've learned that I can't control how people react to my work. All I can do is ask myself, *"What is the message I want to share in this moment?"* and *"How can I share that message as clearly as possible?"* That's all I can do. That's all anybody can do.

Yes, occasionally, people will send bizarre, outraged emails to you at 2:00 a.m. People will call you names. People will misinterpret you and misquote you. People do that.

If you want to be a writer, artist, activist, entrepreneur, community leader, any kind of change-maker—if you want to create anything in a public setting— then enduring judgment and criticism is part of the package deal.

But not everybody will criticize you. Some people will love and appreciate you. Some people will say "Thank you. I needed to read that today," and "The story you just told changed my life," and "You inspired me to keep going."

Just like Paul, Melissa, Susan, and all of the other people featured in this book, you've got to find the courage to keep marching—even when a portion of society doesn't like your face, your website, your ideas, or the very fact that you exist.

Just like Paul, Melissa, and Susan, you've got to stay focused on your friends and your fans. (Yes, even if you only have "two fans" right now.)

Plug those people into your heart. Lock them into your mind. Hold on tight. Remember those people when you're feeling discouraged. Imagine those people encircling you with appreciation. Focus on them. Create for them.

* * *

SURVIVAL TIP:

Christian D. Larson once said, *"Believe in yourself. There is something inside you that is greater than any obstacle."*

It's true. This is the beauty and magic of the human spirit. There is something inside you that is stronger than even the harshest piece of criticism, stronger than the meanest blog comment, stronger than the hate-iest piece of hate mail.

Trust that you have that kind of strength inside of you, because you do. We all do. Yes, you're going to be judged, and yet...you're going to survive.

Chapter Five:

When You Feel Unimportant, Untalented, and Invisible—like Nobody Cares about You, or Your Work Doesn't Matter

IT ALL MATTERS.

When David Wagner's client stepped into his salon and asked him to style her hair, he asked if she had any special plans that night.

"A party, some type of social engagement, anything?"

She said, "No, nothing special."

Which wasn't exactly true. In fact, she did have something planned for that night. Something big.

She was planning to end her life—and she wanted her hair to look nice at her funeral.

David didn't know that, of course. He proceeded to do his work as he always does—with warmth and care, giving a beautiful scalp massage, making his client smile and laugh throughout the process. At the end, they hugged goodbye.

A few days later, David received a letter from that same woman. In her letter, she explained what she'd been planning to do. She said that after seeing David—and after having such a loving, wonderful experience at his salon—she changed her mind at the last moment. Instead of driving home to end her life, she checked herself into a hospital to receive professional care.

In her letter, she thanked David for making a difference in her life.

"Thank you for being there without knowing that you were."

David was so moved by this experience that he went on to write a book inspired by it— *Life As a Daymaker: How to Change the World by Simply Making Someone's Day*— and also he created a website to inspire other people to become Daymakers, too. (It's called DaymakerMovement.com).

I've encountered many religions and spiritual traditions over the years—with many powerful teachings—but no credo has impacted me more deeply than the Daymaker philosophy.

As David puts it:

"Simple acts of kindness can make someone's day and possibly even cause a worldwide ripple effect."

Or, to phrase that a different way, in my own words:

Your words, your actions, your art projects, your efforts, every small, tender, beautiful thing that you put forth into the world matters so much. So much more than you may realize. Every single day, as you go about your work, you have no idea whose life you could be impacting for the better—often, in ways you can't even imagine.

I find it so empowering to remember this fact—to remember how much your efforts matter, especially when you are feeling invisible (*"Nobody is reading my stupid blog"*) or unimportant (*"Nobody wants to give me a book deal"*) or uncreative (*"I don't have any world-changing ideas"*) or boring (*"I have nothing important to say"*) or unsuccessful (*"My business isn't growing;*

My boss didn't give me a promotion; My income is still too low").

You may feel all of these things—invisible, unimportant, uncreative, boring, unsuccessful—but none of these things are actually true. Because if you are willing to make one person's day a little better than it was before—whether it is through a haircut, a compliment, a meal, a blog post, anything at all—then you are making a difference, and you might not realize just how big of a difference you are making.

It could be the biggest difference of all. It could be the difference of inspiring someone to choose life over death. It doesn't get much more important than that.

Remember this power that you hold. Then go do something—big or small, extraordinary or beautifully ordinary—to make another human being's day just a little better than it was before.

What you do matters. Every art project. Every email. Every job, even the jobs you don't love. Every act of care.

It all matters.

* * *

SURVIVAL TIP:

When you're feeling unimportant, untalented, and invisible—like nobody cares about your work—stop for a moment. Pause. Shake your hands. Shake your body. Do some jumping jacks or push-ups or swirl around in your office chair.

Then remind yourself, *"My work does matter. My life does matter. For someone in this world, I can be a Daymaker."*

Then get back to work—and make someone's day a little better than it was before.

Whether you're making coffee, sweeping the floor, writing a blog post, editing someone's cover letter, or ordering lunch for your boss and her colleagues, you have an opportunity, right now, to be a Daymaker. You are much more powerful and influential than you might think.

Be a Lighthouse.

When Maggie Reyes started her blog, she had exactly zero readers. OK, not zero. She had one reader. Her sweet husband.

"You can do it, babe!" he said.

"I know I can!" she said.

Modern Married—Maggie's blog about falling in love, staying in love, and *"creating a life that you love with the love of your life"*—was born.

Maggie started blogging and posting inspirational love-notes on Facebook—notes which, initially, were read by basically no one.

I asked Maggie, "How did you find the motivation to keep writing even though nobody was paying attention at first? Most people get discouraged and quit when they feel 'invisible'. But you didn't. You stuck it out. How come?"

She told me, "Back at the beginning, I would pretend that I was a lighthouse beaming light and love out into the world. I would pretend that thousands of people were listening. I wrote 'as if' thousands of people were listening. I never missed a single blog post because I'd be letting thousands of people down! I imagined that I was changing thousands of people's lives by sharing my ideas every day."

"And eventually," she continued, "A few people started seeing what I was doing. They started sharing it with their friends. Then a few more. And a few more. Word spread. And now, a few years later, *I am that lighthouse!*"

Today, *Modern Married* has a community of over twenty-five thousand appreciative readers and Facebook fans. Maggie was named one of "the relationship experts to watch" by The Gottman Institute—an award-winning company that collects data about marriage and divorce. She's been quoted in publications like *Brides* magazine and *Martha Stewart Weddings*. She also runs a thriving practice as a life and relationship coach. It's her absolute dream job—she gets paid to help couples stay in love and build even stronger, happier marriages. How cool is that?

Maggie is officially living her dream—and it all happened because she decided to operate "as if" the world was already listening.

The moral of this story is pretty darn clear:

If you want to be successful...if you want to be respected in your field...if you want to build an appreciative fan base for your work...or get tons of clients...then you have to operate "as if" the world is already listening.

You have to perform like a musician rocking out to a packed stadium, even if—in reality—you're playing to an audience of two drunk guys who are Tindering on their phones and barely paying attention.

You don't build a fan base by complaining, or by giving a half-hearted performance. You build a fan base by performing full out. Lighthouse of love. Full blast. from day one. Just like Maggie did. Just like she still does.

* * *

SURVIVAL TIP:

Don't complain about "not having enough fans." That's totally unproductive. Instead, decide that you're going to be a lighthouse—beaming love, positivity, great ideas, and awesomeness into the world.

Beam, beam, beam. Shine, shine, shine. Show up and do your thing—post your article, sing your song, give your seminar, teach your class—acting "as if" you've already got thousands of fans. Even if you don't.

One by one, the people who need what you're writing, saying, baking, or making will show up, gathering to bask in your light.

How Can I Make This Feel Amazing?

I've taught writing workshops in eighteen cities around the world, and in all kinds of venues—inside converted barns and farmhouses, yoga studios, publishing companies, people's living rooms and backyards, and one time, on a cruise ship.

Typically, these workshops include creative writing exercises, coaching, conversation, beautiful food, music, and fun surprises—like yoga classes, guided meditations, or an impromptu ukulele performance.

And typically, these workshops fill up pretty quickly. Some go from "empty" to "sold out" in just a few days— or even just a few hours.

Typically.

But not always.

One time, I decided to put together a workshop in my hometown of Los Angeles. It was going to be a summer workshop. A beautiful venue near the ocean. Catered meals. Total perfection. I'd been on a real "winning streak" lately. All of my workshops were completely sold

213

out—or very close. I figured this new workshop would be
no exception.

I put together the webpage. I wrote an announcement
for my blog and newsletter mailing list. I reached out to
some friends in LA to ask if they would spread the word.
The official announcement went out, and...

Almost no one signed up.

A week went by. Three people signed up. Another week
went by. Three more people signed up. Another week
went by. Nothing.

The workshop was approaching quickly. I had a total
of six registrations, and I'd been hoping for twenty or
twenty-five.

It felt really embarrassing.

I agonized over what to do next. Should I cancel or
reschedule the workshop due to low sales? Should I do
a more assertive "push" with my marketing to try to fill
those remaining spaces? I felt rejected and confused.
Why weren't people interested in coming? Did I do
something wrong? Did I choose the wrong dates, the
wrong venue, the wrong topic? I'd never experienced this
type of non-interest before.

I printed out the list of six registered guests. I looked at
the six names over and over again. These six people had
paid hard-earned money to sign up. They had cleared
their calendars for the workshop dates. Some were
traveling from San Diego and San Francisco to be there.

Most likely, many of those people had already booked hotel rooms in Los Angeles.

All six people had said, through the action of registering for the event, *"Hey Alex, I will rearrange my life to be there. I will show up for you."*

Canceling the workshop, at this point, would be completely disrespectful.

They'd promised to show up for me, and I needed to show up for them too—regardless of how full (or not full) this workshop was going to be. This wasn't about money. This was about integrity. So, I made a gut decision. I decided to be completely honest. I emailed the six guests and I said:

> *Hey everyone! Here's the situation:*
>
> *Ticket sales are unexpectedly low. This workshop is still pretty empty.*
>
> *So, please, if you wish, bring along a friend, a partner, your son or daughter, your mom or dad. Bring two friends if you want. Totally free of charge.*
>
> *It's my pleasure to give extra 'complimentary' tickets to all of you.*
>
> *Let's fill this workshop with people we love—and make it a fabulous party that we'll all remember and enjoy.*

All six people were ecstatic and immediately invited all kinds of fascinating people.

"That's so generous!" they exclaimed. "This is amazing!"

Interestingly, the very next day, several people purchased tickets on my website, too. (Unrelated—or not? Payback for good karma? I don't know. But that's what happened.)

When the workshop rolled around, it was a completely full house. About half of the people there were paying guests, and the other half had received free tickets. Every single person was thrilled to be there. And, because of the unique way that this particular workshop came together, the crowd was unusually eclectic.

We had a champion swing dancer in the room. He gave everyone a dance lesson during our lunch break.

We had a male nurse who was a pregnancy and birthing expert in the room, too, and his story was utterly fascinating.

We had best friends, moms and teenage kids, artists, vocalists, illustrators, professional writers, and people who had never written more than emails before. We had entrepreneurs, corporate leaders, full-time parents, and people in between careers.

When the workshop was over, nobody wanted to leave. People stayed, we broke out a few bottles of wine, talked, swapped emails and phone numbers, and did Tarot card readings around the table for hours and hours.

It was the most fun, meaningful, and memorable workshop I've ever experienced—truly, a peak moment for my entire career.

And to think...

I almost canceled the whole thing because I felt hurt and embarrassed about the fact that ticket sales were lower than I'd hoped. I'm so glad I came to my senses.

I often think back to that experience whenever I'm feeling disappointed because something isn't panning out the way I predicted or wanted.

The question I ask myself is:

"How can I make this feel amazing?"

If ticket sales are slow and I feel sad about that, how can I make this feel amazing?

If everyone flakes out at the last minute and only two people show up for my birthday party, how can I make this feel amazing?

If my last publisher says "no thanks" to my new book project (which happened to me—twice), what's the next move? How can I bring my book into the world in a different manner? How can I make this feel amazing?

When we're willing to be imaginative and flexible, there's always some way to turn a sour, disappointing experience into a better experience. Maybe even an amazing experience. Maybe even something better, sweeter, and more emotionally rewarding than whatever you'd originally planned on.

* * *

SURVIVAL TIP:

What's the most frustrating thing you're dealing with in your life or career right now?

Did your job interview get canceled at the last moment? Feeling disappointed? Well, now you've got an open afternoon and some unexpected free time. What's the plan? How could you make this feel amazing?

Did you launch a new project but it's not selling very well? Feeling bummed out? Well, now you've got a big stockpile of that product. What are you going to do with it? Donate product samples to a local hospital or school? Throw yourself a party and give your product away to all your friends? How could you make this feel amazing? How could you make the best of it?

"How do I want to feel about this?" is another great question.

Is this a failed conference with not enough attendees—or a successful dinner party filled with wonderful, intimate conversations? It can be either one. It all depends on how you decide to think about it.

GO BACK IN.

Story contributed by: Ellen Fondiler.
Entrepreneur. Cofounder of MEarth, a nonprofit environmental educational center for kids.

A Note from Alexandra:

If you open a dictionary and search for the word "Persistent," really, you ought to see a picture of my friend Ellen Fondiler.

When there's something she's passionate about—whether it's opening a bakery, starting her own landscape design company, convincing a celebrity to speak at her gala event, or raising millions to build a new educational center for kids in her community—she's like a bulldog with a bone. She will not quit. She will not let go.

This is a story about one of Ellen's toughest challenges—trying to convince a stern, unenthusiastic school board to believe in her project. She felt shocked when they initially said "No." She wondered, *"Why on earth would they reject this idea? Why don't they care about this project?"* She felt rattled—but she didn't give up.

This is the story of what she said to herself (and to her team) in that bleak moment when it seemed like they'd failed.

Ellen is a role model for me, and also, she's not superhuman. She's not a billionaire. She doesn't have five zillion Facebook fans. She's not a world-famous whatever-dee-doodle. She's a regular person. To me, that's the most inspiring part of all. If Ellen can find the courage to keep working and be persistent, then why not me? Why not you? Why not any of us?

* * *

Ellen: I never planned to become an "environmental steward" or a "science educator" or a "nonprofit director." But for a decade of my life, that's exactly what I did and who I was.

It all started with a newspaper article.

While flipping through the weekend section one Friday afternoon, I came across an article about two people who had developed a curriculum for school gardens for elementary schools—a place where kids could learn about plants, flowers, bugs, and natural sciences in a hands-on way, digging around and getting their fingers in the dirt.

I was not an avid gardener. I had never grown my own vegetables or herbs. In fact, at that point in my life, watering an indoor plant was the full extent of my "horticultural experience."

Yet, reading that article, I felt a jolt in my body. I felt so curious and energized.

"Could I build something like that at my kids' school, too?" I wondered.

Turns out—I could.

There was a workshop that very weekend which I immediately signed up for. I read books, took classes, consulted with experts, and taught myself how to set up a garden. I called the principal at my kids' school and asked if I could take a crack at building a garden on campus—purely as a volunteer, no charge at all. She told me to go for it. I happily dove in.

I got my son's teacher excited about the gardening project. Then another teacher. And another. My passion continued to build. Word spread. Before I knew it, I had all the teachers in the school trained up and ready to go. Parents chipped in small amounts of money to keep the garden going, five or ten dollars at a time. Later, we collaborated with local chefs to start a healthy eating program inside the school. Alice Waters—a famous chef and a pioneer in the organic food movement—came to visit, which was such an honor. We were thriving.

A few years after that, a teacher from the local middle school and I decided to expand the small native garden he had planted next to the school into a full-blown eco-habitat— replete with a vegetable and native plant garden and a bird sanctuary. We raised enough money to cover the construction costs and to hire a few people. With a small team—and a gigantic dream—MEarth's story began.

Our vision was simple: we wanted to build an environmental educational center that would serve children for generations to come. A beautiful place that kids from all the surrounding school districts could visit—at no cost—to see where their food came from, learn how to care for our delicate planet, and become good stewards of the environment.

A few years passed, and while we were extremely successful, we found ourselves wanting to expand our programming. We wanted to serve students from all over the county—especially those in underserved areas that did not have the same access to science programs as the kids in our school district. We did a bunch of research, and it became clear that the best way to do this would be to start a nonprofit that would run alongside our existing programs.

Our biggest hurdle? We needed the local school board's approval to use their land and teaching staff before we could move forward—and this school board was notoriously skeptical and difficult to impress.

My team and I worked hard to prepare our presentation. We put together all the documents that had been requested. We thought we had our ducks in a row.

But once we walked into that school board meeting, it became obvious that there had been a major miscommunication between the superintendent and the board. They'd been given the wrong information about our project and had already made up their minds to refuse our request. We were broadsided and did not know if we had been purposely betrayed or if it was just a communication snafu. After a frustrating hour-long debate, the board flatly told us "No."

We couldn't believe it. They were shutting us down— just like that? We wanted to do something beautiful:

build a habitat and educational program for kids! This would change kids' lives! Why wouldn't they give us their blessing?

The next morning, my team and I sat around our conference table, sadly bemoaning what could have been.

As the project leader, I felt more wounded and humiliated than anyone. The whole situation felt like a crushing rejection. But I was unwilling to let our dream fizzle away after one disappointment.

I told the group, "We're going back in. We're not taking 'no' for an answer."

Everyone knew our chances were slim. We were going to present the same idea to the same group of people—who had already firmly rejected it.

But we knew that our project was important. We knew our garden would help thousands of children every year. We couldn't just bow our heads and shuffle away in defeat. Not like this.

First, we did our homework and found out exactly what had happened to cause the communication breakdown between us, the superintendent, and the school board. We smoothed over all the rattled feelings and bruised egos.

Then we went back in. We retold our story to the board, took responsibility for the past confusion, showed them our passion, and won the day.

It was a turning point for our scrappy little organization—and a major life lesson for me. That lesson? If you've been rejected or turned away, you have several options:

—You can accept it and sulk away. ("Oh well, so much for that idea...")

—You can accept it and try to give it a positive spin. ("I guess it wasn't meant to be!")

—Or you can decide that you're not accepting "No" for an answer. You can put yourself back into the arena. You can choose to go back in.

If you choose to go back in, that means...you keep fighting. You try again. You circle back with a better plan, a stronger proposal, a more enticing package, or a more compelling story. You refuse to let one "No" shut down your dream.

Going back in requires courage and nerves of steel, creativity, and resilience. I'm not saying it's the easy option. But for certain projects, it can feel like the only real option.

If I had accepted the school board's initial decision without a fight, I don't think I would have been able to sleep at night. I owed it to my donors, to my team, to the kids in our community, and to myself, to try again.

I've learned that every door can be unlocked—but it doesn't always open on the first try.

Be willing to try again.

Incredible things can happen when you muster up the courage to go back in.

* * *

SURVIVAL TIP:

If you're feeling unwanted or rejected, like nobody cares about your book/blog/project/dream/etc., you can accept defeat.

Or, like Ellen, you can decide to go back in.

Not sure which path to take?

Imagine your personal hero is sitting down with you, having coffee, or sharing a croissant. Someone you really admire. Michelle Obama. Elizabeth Warren. Dr. Martin Luther King, Jr. RuPaul. Pretend you're having a conversation with that person. Tell her (or him) all of your frustrations, everything you're feeling, and ask for their advice.

"What do you think—should I walk away from this project, or keep trying? Should I go back in?"

What do you think your hero would say to you?

Whatever they'd say...do that.

Please Don't Cancel.

This is incredibly embarrassing for me to say, but I'll just say it...

One time, I wanted to cancel a big speaking engagement because I thought I looked "a little too chubby." You know, maybe five or ten extra pounds over my usual weight.

I knew they'd be filming the event and I didn't feel ready to appear on camera.

"Maybe next year...I'll be ready." I caught myself thinking those words. I knew, in that moment, how completely ridiculous I was being. My mind was like a runaway train heading straight into body-shame-hell and I needed to jump off.

Intellectually, I know that I am allowed to step onstage— and that I deserve to be seen and heard—whether I weigh ninety pounds or nine hundred pounds. It makes no difference.

Intellectually, I know that I am creative, talented, beautiful in all the ways that matter, and that my stories matter, too. Because we all have stories that matter. Intellectually, I know all of these things.

And also, I am a human being with human emotions, not a steel-plated confidence-machine. Sometimes, my thoughts go a little screwy.

Sometimes, there's a part of my brain that whispers, *"Have I reminded you lately that...you suck? No? Oh, well...I just wanted you to know."*

Our brains can trick us, sneaking in with insidious thoughts at the most inconvenient moments. You know, like the night before you're supposed to speak in front of four hundred people. Thanks a lot, brain!

Here's what I've learned about myself:

Whenever I'm stepping up to a new challenge, my brain always tries to convince me to wait until "later." My brain tries to convince me that I'm not "thin/fit/strong enough" yet, that I don't have "enough time," or that "next summer would be better."

No. Next summer would not be better. Next summer will come along with its own set of rationalizations and excuses. The right time is right now.

I'm proud to say that I didn't cancel that speaking gig. I really wanted to, but I didn't. I talked myself through that bleak, bizarre moment of body-loathing. I put on my favorite outfit. I got onstage and I told my story. It went great. Better than I'd expected. And then I stepped offstage and I cried with relief.

Afterwards, a few people came up to me to say, "Thank you so much for saying what you said. Your story meant a lot to me."

I thanked them for coming. Privately, I thought to myself, *"And to think...I almost canceled this whole thing. Thank God I didn't."*

Whatever you're about to cancel or postpone—I know there's something—please don't. Just don't. Be brave and charge forward.

Who cares if you've got a pimple? Who cares if your body doesn't look like a Victoria's Secret model? Who cares if your master's degree isn't finished yet? Who cares if your website isn't completely perfect yet? If there's a project that you want to complete—a project that's going to touch people's hearts, change people's minds for the better, or help people feel stronger and less alone—then the world needs your project *now*.

Please don't delete yourself. Please don't flake out. Please don't cancel. Not for any reason, and especially not because of how you look, or how you think you're supposed to look.

Don't let the mean voices inside your head win. Let love win. Let art win.

Finish your project and stop the pattern of canceling on yourself.

Canceling is officially canceled.

* * *

SURVIVAL TIP:

No. More. Canceling.

If you have a pattern of quitting, flaking out, or canceling on yourself, summon all of your inner grit and strength, and decide, "Not this time."

Show up for the audience members who need to hear your story, who will feel less alone once they hear what you've been through. Show up for the colleagues who are counting on you. Most of all, show up for yourself.

He's Waiting. She's Listening.

My very first blog was called *Unicorns For Socialism*—a name that, to this day, still makes no sense to me, or anybody else. I can't remember what compelled me to purchase that particular domain name, but I did, and I set up a basic WordPress site. Off I went into the wild, blue blog-o-verse, ready to share my Various Thoughts and Feelings with the world.

On *Unicorns For Socialism*, I wrote about anything and everything: my favorite TV shows, apple-bran muffin recipes, poetry, manifestos, my thoughts on freelancing, and occasionally, tips on how to communicate more clearly and expressively. It was quite a jumble-tumble of ideas.

Some days, I felt really proud of my writing. Other weeks, I thought everything I posted was absolute garbage. I was experimenting, testing, honing, working out my opinions on all kinds of topics. I was building my voice as a writer, and simultaneously trying to build my career, and, you know, figure out my life.

Many days, blogging felt tedious and depressing because I knew that nobody was reading my work. Well, not "nobody." My dad read everything I posted. (Thanks dad!) But aside from my dad, not many people were showing up to my website. Compared to some of my friends—extremely famous bloggers with thousands of adoring fans—I felt very small and insignificant. I felt like my work didn't really matter.

I kept plugging along, but inside, that quiet, hungry voice kept wondering,

"Is anybody listening?"

Because what's the point of all this effort if nobody is listening?

One morning, I woke up and checked my email. I noticed an unfamiliar name in my inbox.

It was an email from a woman I'd never met. She lived thousands of miles away.

She was a foster-mom. She introduced herself and explained that her daughter was a big fan of my blog.

"Wait, what?" I remember thinking. *"I have...a fan? Like, a fan who's not...my dad?"*

I continued reading the email. This woman explained that her foster-daughter was struggling to make friends at her new school. She told me her daughter loved my blog posts, particularly one post I had written about how to spark up conversations with strangers.

"She reads every article on your website and writes down some of the things you say, and some of the advice you give, and keeps them in a notebook for inspiration and motivation."

This woman also shared with me that her foster-daughter is a survivor of violent abuse. Unspeakable, nightmarish abuse. Slowly, with the support of her new family, this young woman is healing and courageously rebuilding her life.

This woman asked if I would write to her daughter to give her some encouragement. She told me:

"She really looks up to you and you help her so much. So here is the favor I want to ask you: would you please write her a message? She would love that and she really needs something nice."

At this point my laptop was soaked with tears. I was shaking and sobbing uncontrollably. (I am crying right now, reliving that moment. No matter how many times I write or tell this story, I can't tell it without crying.)

I emailed her back to say, "Of course. I'd be happy to do that." (Her daughter and I have been pen pals ever since.)

Reading that mom's email, I realized what a huge fool I had been.

I'd been so concerned about getting famous and getting more readers, more comments, more visible indications of my awesomeness, and all the while, I'd completely forgotten what actually matters. My priorities had been all out of whack. I'd forgotten the entire point of writing and blogging, which is...*to help people*.

On that day, I realized something that changed my entire life:

If I write something—and if my words help *one human being* to have a slightly better day, or a slightly better life—then my writing is a success.

It doesn't matter if I have one thousand readers. It doesn't matter if I get one hundred comments. What matters is helping one living, breathing human being. One person. One life.

I've talked to so many people from so many different industries—writing, music, fashion, health and wellness—who feel invisible and unimportant. People who think, *"I'm not that famous. People barely know about me. I'm not really leaving an impact."*

You might feel that way. And you might be completely wrong about that.

Your work might be impacting people's lives in ways you don't even know about.

That's the reason we have to keep writing, blogging, singing, making videos, speaking up, and starting all kinds of projects, even if it seems like "nobody is listening." Because...somebody always is.

To somebody out there, you might be a role model, a hero, or an uplifting presence in the center of a very bleak day. You might be all of those things and more.

Trust that your work matters because it always does.

Trust that helping one person is enough because it always is.

Keep going because somebody is always waiting for your next piece of art to be released—even if you don't have any comments or fan mail to prove it.

Imagine a teenage girl, fiercely fighting against the horrors of the world, or a mother, searching for encouragement, or a father, trying to be his best, or a son, seeking guidance to get through a trying time.

Imagine that one person. Hold that one person in your heart and dedicate your work to him or her. Let your work be a gift—an expression of care, love, helpfulness and beauty for that one person.

He's waiting. She's listening.

* * *

SURVIVAL TIP:

Even if you only have a tiny handful of fans, clients, or customers right now, that doesn't mean your work is "pointless." Not at all. Those two, three, or four people are being impacted by your work. Those two, three, or four people are going to have a better, happier, slightly less painful day because of something *you* created.

That's a big deal. You're creating a positive ripple effect in each of their lives. That ripple effect could be bigger than you'll ever fully know.

"No act of kindness, no matter how small, is ever wasted." —Aesop

Chapter Six:

When You Feel Tired, Shlumpy, Frumpy, and Unmotivated— like Achieving Your Goal Is "Just Too Hard," or It's Going to Take "Forever"

EXCUSES OR PROGRESS.

I hopped in a cab. The driver and I started chatting, as you do. She asked what I do for work. I told her that I'm a writer. Her eyes lit up.

"That's so cool! My son wants to be an author."

"Oh yeah? What does he like to write about?" I asked.

She explained that her son Ryder is twelve years old. He has declared that he will finish his first novel by his thirteenth birthday. It's a story about twin siblings—a brother and a sister—with supernatural powers. He works on it every single day. Any chance he gets.

Recently, Ryder got in trouble during science class because he was writing story ideas in his notebook instead of paying attention to the teacher. Another time, a different teacher scolded him and said, "Kids don't write books." (Can you imagine?) But none of that has stopped him.

"We don't have a computer at home," his mom, Traci, explained. "It broke a long time ago." Totally dead. Won't even turn on. Sizzled black screen. She's saving money to buy a new one. But it hasn't happened yet.

But for her son? That's no problem. He goes to the school computer lab during lunch—and then again after school—and that's when he works on his novel.

Every day, he pushes himself to finish his homework as quickly as possible so that he can work on his novel. He's been doing this for months.

We arrived at my apartment. I scribbled my contact info and a publishing resource on a scrap of paper and handed it to her. I said goodbye and told her, "You're an amazing mom, and you've got an amazing son."

I've been thinking about this kid ever since. No computer? No problem. Unsupportive teachers? Not an issue. Tons of homework? No sweat. Already finished. This kid is unstoppable. I predict he'll have a trilogy of books—and a movie deal—by the time he graduates from high school.

May we all pursue our dreams with the relentless, undaunted passion of this twelve-year-old kid.

If we applied even one-quarter of his determination to our work, we'd all create miracles.

"Oh but my Internet connection is really slow." "So-and-so hasn't gotten back to me yet." "My assistant is on vacation." "My boss won't let me."

When those voices arise, when you feel like stalling, when the work feels too hard and overwhelming... remember that somewhere in Oregon, there's a twelve-year-old boy named Ryder who's working his butt off at the junior high school computer lab. He's figuring out how to move forward with his goals in spite of every obstacle.

You can make excuses or you can make yourself proud.

You can make excuses or you can make progress.

You can make excuses or you can make art.

Every day, it's your choice.

* * *

SURVIVAL TIP:

In every moment, even when it doesn't feel like it, you are in charge of your life—and your career.

Yes, things are unfair. Yes, computers crash. Yes, people let you down. Yes, all of that. And yet...this is your story, and you're the main character, and you get to determine what happens next. Will you make excuses—or find a way to make progress?

When you're feeling victimized—like you're not in control anymore—try to remind yourself, *"No. That's not true. This is my story, and I determine what happens in the next chapter. If a twelve-year-old kid can write a novel even though he doesn't even own a computer, then I can conquer whatever challenges I'm facing in my own life, too. I can do this."*

Choose Your Purpose.

One time, I got an email from complete stranger on the Internet who wanted to know:

"How can I find my purpose?"

This person felt lost and directionless. So tired of searching, wondering, and not knowing.

I've been there, too. I spent many years comparing myself to my parents (both very high achievers), to my older brother (a Grammy Award-nominated musician), to my younger sister (who has a clear, defined set of passions and interests, unlike me), and to my super-successful friends (who all seemed to have things "figured out").

I wanted to discover my purpose so badly. I would journal, walk, think, vent, meditate, ruminate, and stress about it. Even burst into tears of frustration.

Then one day...I realized that you don't "discover" your purpose. You don't "uncover" it. You don't "find" it.

You just pick something and you do it.

Here's what I mean:

1. Think about something that bothers you.

Maybe "online bullying" bothers you. Maybe "poorly designed websites" bother you. Maybe "animal cruelty" bothers you. Maybe "boring dinner parties" bother you. Maybe "seeing talented people stuck in the wrong type of career" bothers you.

We're all bothered by something. What irritates you? What makes you groan? What breaks your heart?

2. Ask yourself, "What's a cool project that I could do to help 'solve' this issue that bothers me?"

Maybe you could do a fundraiser. Maybe you could write a book to change people's hearts and minds. Maybe you could invent a new product. Maybe you could teach a lunchtime class for your colleagues at work. Maybe you could record a ten-episode podcast series. Maybe you could organize a letter-writing campaign. Come up with a project that sounds interesting to you. Map it out. And then...

3. Promise yourself that you'll complete this project, no matter what.

Completing this project is now...your life's purpose.

That's it.

Get bothered.

Come up with a project.

Work on completing that project.

And then once you've completed that project, then ask yourself, *"OK, what else?"*

Living purposefully can be that simple.

* * *

SURVIVAL TIP:

Stop searching for your purpose. Your purpose isn't something you "find." It's something you "choose." Choose a project that feels interesting to you—and just do it.

"I'm going to find homes for one hundred homeless dogs."

"I'm going to raise two thousand dollars to support a cause that I believe in."

"I'm going to write a book that inspires people not to give up on their dreams."

"I'm going to run a 10K race and then teach other people how to do that, too."

"I'm going to teach fifty local kids how to meditate and release stress in a healthier way."

Pick a project. Complete it. You'll feel proud of yourself. You'll feel purposeful and lit up about life. And then, pick another project. Do that. Continue this pattern until your time on earth is complete.

Keep Marching.

The first time I met Master Phil, I felt completely awestruck. And completely intimidated.

Phil Nguyen—Master Phil, as he's known—is a world-renowned martial arts educator. Think: Bruce

Lee, if Bruce were alive today, and if Bruce ran an awesome blog.

Master Phil radiates a level of devotion and mastery that most people only dream about. He is a 7th Degree Black Belt International Master Instructor in ITF tae kwon do, and also a 1st Degree Black Belt in Kanzenbudo Jiu-Jitsu (because why stop with just one black belt when you can earn two, right?). Along with his wife, he started Bully Busters, an award-winning program that has helped thousands of kids to build assertiveness skills and learn how to respond to bullying confidently and peacefully. His anti-bullying work earned a national commendation from the Queen of England. His first book—*Black Belt Excellence*—debuted as a number one bestseller in the US and Canada. The mayor of his town named him Citizen of the Year. (Please note: this is just a partial, abbreviated list of his many achievements.)

Master Phil is very humble about his work. Nevertheless, it's hard not to feel "small" in his presence.

I was so excited to meet him in person, and yet... meeting him triggered an avalanche of insecurites. I shook his hand with a smile on my face, but inside, I was anxiously wondering...

"Why can't I be disciplined and devoted like him? Why can't I choose one path and stick with it like him? Why can't I be super-amazingly awesome like him?"

And so forth.

Compared to him, I just felt so...pathetic. I didn't say that aloud, of course, but I think he read my mind, because this is what he said next:

"I've been practicing martial arts for thirty years, but I never set out to be a 'master'," he said. "I fell in love with martial arts at age fifteen. I just loved it. And three decades later, here I am. I'm not superhuman or anything. I'm just the kid who kept marching."

And it's true. People like Master Phil, they're no different from you or me. The only difference is that they pick something that they love and decide to keep marching. They're patient. They're tenacious. They wake up every morning and—whatever they're doing—they stand up and do it all over again.

Ten, twenty, or thirty years later? Whoa. Who knows where you could be?

You could see your face on the cover of a magazine. You could be serving your ten-thousandth customer. You could finally have your dream job, the one that took ten years to find and secure, but now here you are. Because you decided to keep marching. And marching. And marching.

* * *

SURVIVAL TIP:

Most of us get so caught up in what we want to be, have, or do...*right now*. Most of us love instant gratification and instant results. But what about ten, twenty, or thirty years from now? What's your long-range dream? Consider that. What could be possible for you if—like Master Phil—you simply decide to keep marching?

500 POSTS.

Story contributed by: Shauna Haider.
Blogger. Artist. Founder of Branch, a design agency.

A Note from Alexandra:

Shauna is a soft-spoken, dark-haired woman who listens more than she talks. If you bumped into her at a party, you might assume she works as a librarian. Like a really sexy, slightly punk rock librarian.

She is not a librarian. She's a talented artist, designer, and entrepreneur, and she runs a tremendously successful blog with an international readership. A readership that includes...me.

I stumbled across Shauna's blog a long time ago—back when I was in college. I was immediately entranced by her gorgeous photos, stylish outfits, and thoughtful posts on design, creativity, collaboration, and how to succeed as a freelancer.

At the time, we lived in different cities, and I never dreamed we'd ever get to meet in real life. But eventually, we did. And she's just as lovely in real life as she seems online.

I asked Shauna, "Can you tell me about the early days of your blogging career, back when you didn't have very many readers? What did that feel like?"

This is her story, and her sensible advice for anyone who's feeling impatient about a blog, a book, a business, or any other type of creative project.

As Shauna points out, it takes time to find your voice and build momentum. Most people quit way too quickly. The people who succeed aren't necessarily more "interesting" or "talented." They're just the people who don't quit.

* * *

Shauna: My very first blog wasn't actually a blog, technically. It was LiveJournal profile. Remember LiveJournal? It was this website where anybody could start a "public diary." You could write about anything you wanted—fashion, music, food, happy moments from your day, or heavier stuff, like struggling with addiction or an eating disorder.

Every LiveJournaler had their own style. Some people wrote exclusively about one topic. Others wrote about all kinds of things. Some people's LiveJournals became really popular—they were sort of like "Internet celebrities," before that was really a "thing."

I loved LiveJournal because it felt so personal. A lot of today's blogs are very slick and polished, but Live Journal was kind of...raw. Nobody was trying to sell anything, or build a huge following, necessarily. It was just real people sharing real feelings, writing about whatever they felt like.

After doing Live Journal for a couple years, I decided I wanted to start my own blog. I called it NubbyTwiglet.

com, inspired by my college nickname. I bought that domain name and I found a free WordPress theme that I paid my friend two hundred dollars to customize. It wasn't bad—there weren't any flashing GIFs or anything like that—but it wasn't exactly a work of art. My first blog looked far from "polished" by today's standards. But I loved it. I felt so excited to have my very own corner of the Internet. It felt pretty fancy.

Of course, I didn't have a huge amount of readers at first. Some, but not a ton. Most of my real life friends were pretty supportive, and some of my online LiveJournal friends followed me over to my new online home and checked things out. But I definitely had moments where I felt discouraged, like, *"Ugh, nobody cares about my dumb blog. Nobody's reading. Not that many people, anyway. Why am I even bothering to do this?"*

Even today, over a decade later, I still feel that way sometimes. I think everyone does—even if they have a massive audience. One of my closest friends has over one million blog readers every month, and even she feels "invisible" sometimes. Sometimes, it can feel like you're posting into thin air...no feedback, no emails, no nothing. Crickets!

When I'm feeling discouraged, my personal strategy is to take a few days off. I try to unplug, avoid the blogosphere, see friends, see art, take a weekend trip out of town, or take a walk outside and get re-inspired. Usually, my excitement returns pretty quickly, and I discover that I've got lots of things to say, and I want to start blogging again.

I'm a strong believer in the mindset of *"slow and steady wins the race."* If you want something to be solid, you have to be in it for the long haul.

There's rarely such a thing as an overnight success. The truly great writers and bloggers that I know have been perfecting their craft for years. It takes probably five hundred posts just to find your voice and solidify your direction, so don't give up too quickly.

I've definitely experienced a lot of moments where I considered giving up. But I'm glad I didn't. My blog has led to so many beautiful things—new friendships, new clients, opportunities to travel (and get paid for it), opportunities to teach and create classes, all kinds of things that probably never would've happened if I'd quit blogging a long time ago. So my advice to you is...*don't quit*. Whether it's a blog, or some other project, try to be patient. We're all in such a hurry, but some projects take time and persistence. Who knows what kinds of opportunities could be waiting for you ten blog posts from now, or ten months from now, or one hundred tries from now? It could be magical. But you'll never find out if you quit now.

* * *

SURVIVAL TIP:

Be patient. Be patient. Be patient.

Like Shauna points out, it can take five hundred blog posts before you feel like you've really hit your stride.

Malcolm Gladwell says it takes ten thousand hours to truly master your craft, whether it's writing, basket-weaving, or managing a team.

Mark Ruffalo went on six hundred auditions before he booked his first acting gig.

Chicken Soup for the Soul, one of the top-selling book series of all time, was rejected by 144 publishers.

We all want success, rewards, and caramel-laced chocolate bars *right now.* Or ideally, *yesterday!* But sometimes, success requires persistence and long-term devotion.

What kind of person do you want to be? An impatient person who quits after three tries? Or someone like Shauna? Like Mark? You get to decide.

Oh Yes. You Can.

It was the night of my five-year anniversary of being self-employed. My *entrepreneur-iversary,* as I call it.

To celebrate the momentous occasion, I decided to go bouldering—aka, rock climbing without a harness—with my boyfriend. Smart, right?

A few hours later, I was in the emergency room with a broken fibula.

Happy anniversary to meeee!

After breaking my leg, I felt an overwhelming rush of shame and sadness. It felt like a huge setback on so

248

many levels. Even though I was grateful to be alive, and even though I knew my injury would only be temporary, all I could think about was everything I *couldn't do*. I couldn't walk. I couldn't run. I couldn't bike. I couldn't do any of the things I loved to do.

For a while, I couldn't even descend the stairs without supervision. I felt trapped in my apartment, isolated and frustrated. Even the simple act of making a cup of coffee and carrying it over to the couch became a huge, complicated undertaking. (Crutches + hot coffee = spills. So many spills.)

For awhile, I even stopped writing. My heart wasn't in it. I felt like I had nothing to say. That hadn't happened... ever.

One day, shortly after my accident, my friend Justin came over to pay me a visit. Justin is a fitness trainer, and he's one of the strongest people—physically and emotionally—that I know. He brought me a sandwich and plopped on the couch. I immediately started crying. Seeing him—strong, healthy, and vibrant—just reminded me about all of the things I couldn't do. All of my limitations. All of my "can'ts."

"You know," he said, as if reading my mind. "As soon as you feel ready, I could plan some workouts for you. I have a lot of experience working with injured people. We can figure out some moves that you can do safely."

"Really?" I sniffled.

"Totally."

After getting the OK from my doctor, I got back into the gym. Turns out, Justin was right. There were plenty of things I couldn't do with a broken leg—but there were a lot of things that I could do. Much more than I realized. I could do one-legged deadlifts. I could do one-legged push-ups. I could do one-legged battle ropes. Even one-legged rowing on the rowing machine! There's a whole lot of stuff you can do with two arms and one leg! Who knew?

Slowly, with each passing day, the track looping inside my mind shifted from *"I can't"* to *"I can...I can...I can."*

Those workouts with Justin taught me a valuable lesson:

I can't always do "everything" I want right this second... but I can always do "something."

No time to write a book because you are raising three kids? Write a haiku.

No cash for a luxurious island vacation with your sweetheart? Give her one deep, long kiss and make it count.

No energy to pour into your marketing plan for your business right now? Send one email to one customer who bought something, anything, from you in the past ten years to say, "Thank you for believing in me." Call it good.

You can always do *something*. It might be small. It might not be sexy, flashy or glamorous. But you can take one step—one awkward, hobbly, crutch-hoppy step—to move one inch closer to having the career you want to have, or becoming the person you want to be.

* * *

SURVIVAL TIP:

Even if you only have one workable leg, or one hour, or ten minutes to spare, there's got to be *something* you can do to work towards your goal.

Maybe you can't do everything today, but you can do something. You can always do something. Today...what's it going to be? Choose something, commit, and just do it.

True Home.

It was summertime. My hair was long and loose. I had recently discovered how to apply black eyeliner with impeccable precision, and my summer-look was one-part Cleopatra, one-part modern Bohemian goddess. Neon colored nails. Big earrings. High hopes.

I was in the midst of a multi-city tour, teaching writing workshops all across the country. I'd recently moved away from Minneapolis. My life was in boxes, suitcases, and shipping containers. I was in between worlds. I had no permanent address, no pets, no tethering responsibilities of any kind. I had enough work, but not too much. I was single. I was free. I was open to any and all possibilities.

Then a guy sat down next to me. Let's call him "Logan."

It was late. I was enjoying a cold beer at a nondescript bar in the far northern tip of Portland, Oregon. I was writing, typing away on my laptop, lost in my thoughts. Then I felt someone settle onto the barstool next to mine. He, too, opened up his laptop and began typing. Inevitably, eyes met, looks were exchanged, and we started talking.

"What are you working on?" he asked.

"A blog post. Something for a client. What about you?"

"A blog post. My personal blog."

"What's it about?" I asked.

A pause. Logan smiled, looked away for a moment, as if deciding how much to reveal.

"Honestly? It's a blog about my divorce. It's anonymous. I am writing about relationships, sex, things like that. All the things I'm feeling right now."

I took a sip of my beer.

"Cool."

We stayed and talked until the bartender flicked on the lights and nudged us out the door. We walked and talked more until Logan noticed an old building with a ladder leading up to the roof. We climbed up the scaffolding and found ourselves on a tiled ledge, side-by-side, looking into the night sky. I pressed my feet nervously into the ledge to prevent myself from slipping off. I tried to smile and act relaxed, like trespassing and climbing onto rooftops with mysterious strangers was just part of my nightly routine. No big deal.

He kissed me. It was one of the best kisses of my life.

I fell in love with Logan, quickly and wildly, with my heart wide open. The next several weeks became a haze of incredible adventures. We scampered all over town, under bridges, at nightclubs, finding excitement at every turn. I wrote poetry about him. I told everyone about him. I scheduled my work and my life to suit his convenience. Why not? It felt right. Anything and everything: all for him.

To his credit, Logan repeatedly warned me not to get too close. His divorce was barely finalized. His ex-wife still had belongings at their old house. Her hair was still caught in his old hairbrushes. That expired yogurt in the fridge: probably hers. Understandably, he didn't want to start dating anyone seriously, not yet. He wanted to feel free. He liked me, sure, he wanted to see me, sure, but he wanted to see other women, too.

I tried to play it cool.

I tried to understand.

But when you're already tumbling off the rooftop, you can't stop your descent in mid-fall. I couldn't "pause" or "reverse" my deepening feelings for him. I was falling fast and hard. It was too late to float back up to safety.

One night, while I was out of town for a brief business trip, Logan asked if we could talk. I ecstatically agreed.

We logged onto Skype. He looked gorgeous as usual, and my heart fluttered and reverberated in my chest. He asked about my trip. I asked about his life. He told me, with a sweet smile, that his week was going awesomely because he had a fantastic date with a woman that he's really attracted to. She was beautiful and smart. They had a great time. He couldn't wait to see her again.

I stared blankly into the screen. I couldn't breathe. My stomach lurched.

Is this really happening? Is this his way of not-so-subtly "reminding" me that I'm not the only woman in his life? Is he a complete idiot with no regard for my feelings? Am I a complete and utter idiot?

"Are you OK?" he asked.

"No, I am not OK. I feel jealous and sad. I wish I didn't feel that way, but I do."

I knew Logan wasn't doing anything wrong. He'd always been honest with me about his intentions. He wasn't being intentionally cruel. He was just living his life—doing his best to navigate the upheaval of his post-divorce world, trying to figure out who he was and what he wanted and where to go from here. He was a newly single man, enjoying his freedom, exploring his options, savoring an unfettered chapter in his life. He had every right to do so.

Nothing about his journey was "wrong."

But it was a journey that I could not continue to participate in.

A few days later, I asked Logan if we could meet in person. He agreed and then canceled at the very last moment. I felt hurt and told him so. He told me I was being ridiculous. We exchanged a few bitter text messages and then rescheduled.

Finally, we set a date to meet in a public park.

He arrived before me. I saw him lying outstretched on the grass. The light was soft. Everything was golden and green, mostly warm, but with the faintest nip in the air. Summer was over.

I walked over. He smiled. We sat close. I pulled out a letter that I had typed and printed at home. As we sat in the grass, I read the letter explaining why I needed to stop seeing him, why staying friends would be too painful for me, and how I was ready and open to meet the love of my life—a permanent, forever-love—and while I wished that person could be Logan, evidently, that person was going to be someone else.

After I finished reading, he pulled me into a tender hug. For a few moments, we said nothing. Then he told me, "You deserve that kind of love, and I have no doubt that you will find it."

I wiped away a few tears and said, "I know I will."

I stood up, waved goodbye, turned away, and walked to my car without glancing back. Inside my car, I pulled out my phone and deleted Logan's phone number and email.

I felt strong, powerful, and optimistic.

I also worried I would never meet anyone as amazing as Logan ever again. Worried that I would never feel emotions that deeply again. Worried, but still hopeful.

I met a girlfriend named Pixie for tea. I filled her in on the whole story. I told her that all I wanted was to meet someone who loved me in the same way that I loved them. Mutual love-splosion. She listened to my story, sipped her beverage, and confidently declared: "You are ready to meet your king. Logan was close, possibly, but he wasn't your king. But don't worry. He's coming. You are calling in your king."

It sounded kinda woo-woo and mystical, but I got it. I nodded. I believed her. I could feel it—that strange, tingling awareness of invisible things, like when you wake up a split-second before your alarm clock goes off, or when you sense that the phone is about to ring and then it does. Someone was coming. My person, the love of my life...was close. I could feel it.

I was right.

Brandon arrived in my life just a few months later. Once again, I fell in love quickly and wildly, with my heart wide open. Once again, life became a haze of incredible adventures with excitement at every turn. But this time, there was one key difference, which is that Brandon and I longed for the same things in life—not different things.

The love that I share with Brandon is unlike anything I've ever experienced. It sounds like a cheesy pop ballad, but truly, I've never known a love like this before.

Back when I met Logan—and when I learned that he was unwilling to be monogamous—I felt rejected and pierced to my very core. I wondered if I wasn't beautiful enough. I wondered if I wasn't interesting enough. I wondered why, why, why, why I wasn't "enough" for him. Why I couldn't satisfy him. It was the most crushing rejection I've ever experienced because I saw so much potential for us, if only, you know, he could change all of his feelings and become a different person. (Small details.)

When you're wallowing in that type of pain, it's like a fog that obscures everything around you. You can't think. You can't see. You tend to experience a type of temporary amnesia. You forget that this person—the person who doesn't want you in the way you want to be wanted—is *not the only person on the planet*.

In reality, there are seven billion other people on the planet. There is someone else for you. Possibly, someone incredibly near and close. Your king or queen could be right around the corner, sitting across the coffee shop, or online right now updating his or her dating profile and searching for someone like you.

Even though it can be difficult, try not to obsess over "the one who got away" or fixate on trying to "make" someone want you. If they don't, then they don't. If they won't, then they won't. Move forward. Take a walk around the block.

You never know who is waiting—sometimes, quite literally—right around the corner.

If I hadn't met Logan during that gypsy-boho-summer when I had no permanent home address, then I might not have stayed in the city of Portland long enough to meet Brandon. I think about this often.

Meeting, dating, and saying goodbye to Logan initiated a chain reaction of serendipitous events that ultimately culminated with me in bed, tangled in sheets and hope and amazement, with a beautiful man in my arms, so warm and close in the midst of winter with snow falling softly outside, a wood-burning stove, and him whispering, "I love you forever, I want you forever, I love you forever, only you forever..."

The rejection you're experiencing today could be a stone rolling down, down, down, creating a domino-sequence of experiences leading you towards a life that is everything you dream about and more.

Your "Logan" could lead to your "Brandon."

Your most excruciating, ego-rattling rejection could lead to finding your true home.

* * *

SURVIVAL TIP:

Rejection hurts. When someone doesn't want to date you, or hang out with you, or collaborate with you, or hire you, or buy into your product, or give you what you want, it hurts. But, try to have some faith.

Whatever you're going through right now could be leading you towards something incredible. Your most exciting project, your new best friend, your true love... who knows what's waiting right around the corner?

If Logan hadn't broken my heart, I probably wouldn't have met Brandon when I did. If Jeff hadn't told me, "You're not getting the job," I probably wouldn't have left the radio broadcasting company and I probably wouldn't have started my own business. If Cathy S. hadn't left that horrible Yelp review, I probably wouldn't have written this book.

All of this pain you're experiencing...maybe it's happening for a reason. Or maybe there's no apparent reason, but you can *create* a reason. You can take this painful mess and turn it into something beautiful. Like the late Carrie Fisher urges us to remember, you can take your broken heart and turn it into art.

What If You Didn't Give Up?

When my brother Ben was a gangly, awkward teenager, he and a couple of his buddies would head to the Third Street Promenade—a popular outdoor shopping area in

Los Angeles—to play music on the street and, hopefully, earn a few dollars.

You can imagine the scene. Shoppers shuffling by clutching bags from The GAP and Old Navy. A handful of teenage boys playing jazz music. An open saxophone case on the ground filled with homemade CDs and loose change.

My brother would screw his eyes tightly shut as he played. When I asked him why, he said, "Pretty girls make me nervous and then I can't remember which notes to play." (He might have been joking. But I don't think he was.)

I remember those Third Street Promenade performances very well.

Do you know what I remember most of all?

I remember watching my brother and his friends play music...to audiences of basically zero.

Occasionally shoppers would stop to listen. But mostly not. My brother and his friends did not get much attention. They did not get much applause. It was a miracle of epic, historic proportions when someone tossed a crumpled five-dollar bill into their case instead of just loose nickels and dimes.

Oh, also, they were not really that "good."

Still, they kept playing.

Let's fast-forward several decades.

Today: my brother is a Grammy-nominated musician and composer. He's regularly profiled in *The New York Times* and he's considered one of most exciting jazz musicians of his generation. He's been called a "striking and distinctive player." Even Snoop Dogg gave him a compliment one time. Is he "good"? Yeah. He's really good. He's a full-time musician, earning a living and living his dream.

Sometimes I wonder...

Way back when...

Back when Ben was a gangly teenager playing tunes on the Promenade...what if he had lost hope? What if—after watching yet another family shuffle by without stopping to listen or tip a few dollars—he had tossed his sax into the case saying, "That's it! I suck. They suck. This all sucks. I'm over it."

What if he had given up?

He could have given up. Most people do. For some reason, he didn't.

What about you?

What will happen if you give up?

(I know you've thought about it. Everybody does.)

What will happen if you give up on your art?

What will happen if you give up on your dream, mission or cause?

How will you feel if you walk away?

How will you feel if you don't?

If there's one thing that is universally true about human beings, it is that we tend to give up far too quickly and too easily. We don't like hard work. We lack patience. We do everything in our power to avoid rejection, disappointment, and humiliation. We don't like to feel emotions that are not "fun" to feel. It's easier to give up. So we do.

But what if you didn't?

What if you chose to be one of the few—one of the very few—who keeps marching?

Who knows where you could be—what you could be enjoying, doing, creating, savoring—five, ten, or fifteen years down the road, if you can just find the grit in your heart to keep going?

It's your call.

You can quit right now. Un-enroll. Hand in your notice. Shut down the website. Pack up your case and go home. Never play a note again. The end.

Or you can decide that following that persistent longing in your heart—the longing to create, to write, to make a difference in the unique way that you feel called to do it—is worth just a little more patience.

You can give up.

Or you can decide that your story is not over yet.

* * *

SURVIVAL TIP:

Think about the career that you want—or the project, book, goal, dream, whatever you're working on. How will you feel if you give up—and how will you feel if you don't?

Write a letter to a friend, but pretend it's ten, twenty, or thirty years in the future. Write your letter "as if" you decided not to give up. You can start your letter with something like this:

"It's been thirty years since I started working on _____, and I'm so glad I didn't give up, because... whoa. Here's what's happened in the last thirty years..."

Then describe all of the beautiful things you've created, experienced, and achieved. Describe the people you've met, and the lives you've been able to touch. Describe the positive ripple effect you've created in your community. The mark you've left on the world. Describe how you feel. The pride and satisfaction in your heart. Describe it all.

Finish writing your letter. Send it to a friend—an actual friend who will read it, and who can hold you accountable to the future-promise you've made.

Then go live that life. Make those choices. Do those things. Don't give up.

Today Is Not Over Yet.

It was a glum, soggy, heart-sagging kind of Saturday. I slept in till noon—and would have slept longer if my boyfriend hadn't rustled me awake.

After a long, tedious drive home through the rain, I was completely exhausted. I looked at my clock. Nearly 3:00 p.m.

"Day's practically over," I thought to myself. My bed was looking pretty damn good. An afternoon nap...a Netflix marathon...maybe a pizza delivery for dinner. Sure. Why not.

"It's not like I'm going to accomplish anything today at this point," I thought, shambling my way over to bed. *"Might as well just flop."*

But then, quite suddenly and dramatically—as if one of my brain lobes spontaneously decided to channel the spirit of Tony Robbins—I heard five words in my mind:

Today is not over yet.

I glanced at my bed one more time. Heard it again.

Today is not over yet.

"OK," I thought. *"New plan."*

This is what happened next:

I went online and I found a yoga class that was happening in about thirty minutes. I signed up. I hauled myself over to the studio. I arrived early, for a change.

I had a beautiful conversation with my teacher. We smiled. We laughed.

After the class, I decided to ring up the local community wellness center. Could they slide me in for a massage at the very last moment? Miraculously: they could. I got the best massage of my life. I soaked in a Jacuzzi by starlight with raindrops splashing on my face.

After that, I walked home. On the way, I called my mom. More smiling. More laughter.

Back at home, I discovered a new public radio program. I made a nourishing dinner. I wrote letters to my friends. I wrote a blog post. Then another one. I had a brilliant idea for a new class I'd like to teach one day. I wrote it down. Finally, I sank into my bed feeling so...full. So satisfied. So happy.

The soggiest, laziest, most forgettable day of my week became the most beautiful, enriching and memorable day of my month.

It turned on a dime—in one split-second decision—with a simple statement of fact:

Today is not over yet.

So you overslept and missed your morning run? Today is not over yet.

So you had a Diet Coke, two cigarettes and four donuts for lunch?

Today is not over yet.

So you frittered away your time on Facebook, spent mindless hours loitering in your inbox, and procrastinated with smartphone games instead of working on your novel?

Today is not over yet.

If your heart is beating, if your lungs are breathing, if you are still alive...then it is not too late to do something kind, creative, generous, satisfying, and courageous. Today.

It is not too late to behave like the person you want to be—instead of continuing in a cycle of behavior that you will regret.

You might feel sleepy. You might feel lazy. You might feel wounded. You might feel discouraged. It might be tough. It could seem preferable to just sit this one out. But...

Today is not over yet.

Chapter Seven:

Survival Toolkit

A CHECKLIST FOR DARK TIMES.

Oh noooo!

You just got criticized/rejected/shamed/publicly humiliated/fired/not hired/etc.

Or maybe you're just having a shlumpy, mopey kind of day for no particular reason.

I'm sorry. You probably feel gross and terrible right now. I wish I could give you a hug. But we're probably not sitting in the same room, so in this moment, all I can offer you is...this Survival Checklist. I hope it helps a little bit.

Here are twenty-one different things you can do to help yourself feel a little better—inspired by the smart people who contributed stories for this book.

[ ] Vomit your feelings into a private diary without censoring yourself. Burn it later if you want.

[ ] Cry. Soak your pillow with tears. Then punch your soggy tear-filled pillow. It's better to let those feelings out rather than bottle them up.

[ ] Manage the crisis as best you can. Send out a press release. Make a statement. Issue a correction. Send flowers to apologize. Put out the fire in the most dignified, classy manner that you can. (Defensive tone: not helpful.)

[ ] Watch an entertaining TV show—the more scandalous, the better. Try: *unReal, Gossip Girl,* or

Scandal. Or something very soothing like *Gilmore Girls* or *Friends*.

[ ] Work harder. Do better. Sometimes, being criticized is a valuable kick in the pants to help you reach your full potential. Consider: is the criticism justified? Are you really giving your best effort—or making a half-effort? Could you try harder next time?

[ ] Look for the bright spots in the darkness. Maybe ninety-nine people left cruel comments on your photo or blog post. But maybe one person said something sane, humane, and kind. Focus on what's good in the world.

[ ] Get a T-shirt printed with vicious criticism that you've received printed on it. Ha-ha! Now it's a hilarious "inside joke" that you and your closest friends can share. Or maybe it doesn't feel funny at all, in which case...

[ ] Do a flicking visualization. Lie down, close your eyes, and visualize flicking or shaking negative energy away from your body—like you're a soaking wet puppy shaking water off its coat. *Shake-shake-shake.* In your mind's eye, watch the icky negativity get flicked away.

[ ] Do a protective visualization. Lie down, close your eyes, and imagine a force field surrounding you and protecting you. Nothing can penetrate your force field unless you allow it to pass through. Positive vibes only.

[ ] Look at the whole picture rather than one person's isolated opinion. Collect opinions from many sources. Talk to your boss, colleagues, castmates, audience members, reviewers, and look within yourself. Does

everyone have the same piece of criticism to give you? Look for common trends.

[ ] Take a walk. Walk ten thousand steps. Walk across your entire town. Walk until it's dark out. You'll feel very different.

[ ] Indulge in simple pleasures. Chocolate. Tea. A massage. A fun movie. Hang out with someone you love. Detach from your source of pain and try to relax. Yes, your career is important—but it's not the only thing that matters in life.

[ ] Create procedures to prevent this type of crisis from happening again in the future. Do you need stricter boundaries regarding which types of clients you work with? More discernment about who you date? Write new policies for your career and/or your personal life. (Google: "Alexandra Franzen—How to write policies" for some tips.)

[ ] Seek the truth. Maybe someone is accusing you of something that isn't entirely true, but nonetheless, look for the kernels of truth embedded in the situation. What is "true" about how the other person is feeling? What is "true" about how you could help them to feel better?

[ ] Block and delete. Sometimes, you simply need to distance yourself from people who don't understand you and probably never will. Unfriend people on Facebook. Unfollow. Deactivate comments on your blog. It's OK to make your life feel a little safer and quieter.

[   ] Read your love-mail. Create a folder filled with positive emails from friends, family, and happy colleagues/customers, and read those messages when you need a lift.

[   ] BREATHE.

[   ] Coach yourself. Interrupt a negative thought in its tracks. Challenge that thought. Disagree like you're having a heated debate.

[   ] Flip your perspective. Is this a setback or a push forward? Is this a crushing rejection or a breath of fresh air and freedom? What feels like a nightmarish situation right now could ultimately become one of the biggest blessings of your life.

[   ] Change what you can. Accept what you can't. Every time you go online, step outside your house, publish a piece of writing, or stand onstage, you are voluntarily entering into a "conversation" with the world. People are going to have feelings and opinions about you. People are going to react and say all kinds of things to your face, behind your back, and sometimes, in shadowy corners of the Internet.

You can't control every aspect of the conversation. You never will. Accept this. Focus on putting forth your best effort—in whatever career you've chosen—and try to make sure the volume of the conversation "out there" doesn't become louder than the sound of your own mind and heart.

[ ] Remember that every single person in the history
of mankind has experienced criticism, rejection, and
discouragement in their lives and careers. You are not
alone. And you're going to survive.

What's Your Plan Z?

Everyone has a Plan A—the one where everything goes
right, you get the girl (or guy), your novel gets published,
your career is filled with excitement and passion, your
hair is shiny and lustrous, and you end your earthly days
eating goat cheese, honey, and crystallized lavender
petals in an Italian villa with a million dollars in your
savings account.

Most people also have a Plan B—a contingency scenario.
A not-terrific but still-acceptable alternative to the
ecstatic glory of Plan A. It might involve getting a
roommate, taking out a loan, or lining up a part-time job
to cover the bills for awhile.

But what about your Plan Z—the absolute worst case
scenario? The end of the road. The point of no return.
The bottomest bottom. The lowest low. The pit of
despair. EPIC. FAILURE.

Often, we don't like to think about Plan B—let alone Plan
Z. It feels too scary and discouraging to even...go there.

But actually, I find that it's very empowering to write
down my Plan Z. Every awful, terrible detail. Because
writing down my "worst nightmare" can help to strip the
power— and terror—out of the situation.

For me, Plan Z means...

—There's zero money in my bank account.

—My business is tanking. My reputation is in ruins.

—I move into a raggedy studio apartment, which I rent for $200 a month.

—I share the apartment with two complete strangers that I found on Craigslist. One of them is nicknamed "Greasy Joe Daddy" or "Big Red" or something to that effect.

—Instead of working as a self-employed writer / author / writing consultant, I have to get a grim job as a graveyard shift bartender in the dive bar to end all dive bars.

—I sling beer and sing Dolly Parton songs to entertain the bikers who stop by the bar. Sometimes I pop outside for a cigarette. I've never been a smoker before, but this is my Plan Z—so I'm burning through at least a pack a day.

—I wear the same pair of ripped jeans every day. I drink drip coffee from McDonalds. I eat 99-cent packs of Hostess snack cakes.

—At the end of my shift, I trundle home to my empty mattress. I sleep on the floor next to the rat that I've adopted as my pet.

—On my days off, I drink cheap boxed wine and make sandwiches out of Skippy peanut butter and Wonder

Bread, which I eat on the sidewalk as I watch the local kids play jump rope and hopscotch.

—I curl my hair with empty Coke cans—like Lady Gaga in the "Telephone" music video—and stare at gasoline rainbows in gutter puddles.

—My partner Brandon has left me, naturally. So I write poems and song lyrics about my gut-wrenching heartache.

—As a silver lining, now that my career is in shambles, and I have no clients, and so on, I have plenty of free time to write my next novel—which I work on diligently at the local public library, because I no longer own a laptop, tablet, or phone. And the book is coming along nicely.

Once I write it all down...My Plan Z doesn't actually sound that bad.

I mean, is it what I want? Obviously, no. Will I do everything within my power to avoid it? Yes. Is it likely to happen? It's possible, I suppose, but fairly improbable. But even so...if it ended up happening? I know I could survive it.

It would suck. My ego would be bruised. But I could do it. It would be embarrassing, stressful, and lonely, and there would be less Brie and more Kraft Singles. But it would not be fatal.

I've lived in an undesirable apartment before. I've had −$300 (yes, that's a negative symbol) in my checking account before. I've worked not-exactly-wonderful waitressing jobs before. I could do it again, if I really needed to. I would not die.

And who knows? My Plan Z might even lead to some of my best writing—or at the very least, a new level of personal strength, resilience, and empathy for people who are struggling, too. It could be the worst thing ever— and also, in a twisted way, the best thing ever, too.

I urge you to try this. Write your Plan Z in all its wretchedness. Every detail. Every fear. Every shameful scenario. Write it out. Read it back. Then say to yourself,

"My Plan Z will probably never happen. But even if it does, I will still be OK."

Then breathe a huge sigh of relief—and keep marching forward towards the business, the career, the art project, the new chapter, whatever's pulling at your heart, whatever you want.

You have survived. You will survive. You can handle whatever comes next.

And if our plans implode in our faces? Well, come on down and see me at Ol' Grandma Nelly's Dive Bar and Shrimp Shack Emporium, or wherever I end up bartending. I'll meet you there. We'll cry into our tumblers of whiskey. We'll kick on the jukebox. We'll figure out our next move. And then onward we go.

If All Else Fails...
Ten of the "Best Possible" Worst Case Scenarios.

OK, so you've got your Plan A, your Plan B, and maybe (if you read the previous page) your Plan Z. The worst case scenario that you could imagine.

But what if things get *even worse* than your Plan Z? What if things get so awful—like, no home, no friends, not a single cent to your name, absolute despair? That kind of awful?

Well, even if everything falls apart in one horrific tsunami of unthinkable chaos...don't worry! You've still got options. Beautiful ones.

You can always...

Become a Wwoofer

WWOOF stands for "Willing Workers on Organic Farms." It's an international network of farms that you can live on (for free!) in exchange for picking strawberries, tilling the fields, gathering eggs, mending fences and other pastoral pursuits. No farmhand experience required—just a willing mind and body. More info here: wwoofinternational.org

Join the Peace Corps

A monthly living and housing allowance. Full medical and dental coverage. 48 paid vacation days. Yes!

Promoting "world peace and friendship" sounds like a pretty terrific gig. More info here: peacecorps.gov

Live In a Monastery

Craving a life of service and spiritual nourishment? Don't mind waking up the crack of dawn? Many monasteries and nunneries have work/stay programs. Search for opportunities here: volunteermatch.org

Work In a Hostel

While tromping through New Zealand many years ago, I spent a few happy nights at a hostel near Picton Harbor. It had a hot tub surrounded by fragrant pine trees, a chocolate pudding bar (yes, really!) and freshly baked bread every morning. In other words: heaven on earth. When I learned that they allow travelers to work in exchange for lodging, I was tempted to stay indefinitely. If my student visa hadn't run out, I might still be there today! You'll find lots of hostel gigs here: hosteljobs.net

Teach Overseas

Got a college degree? Then you can apply to teach English to kids and grown-ups around the world. You can get placed at a private school, public school, even a refugee camp—and most gigs include housing as part of your compensation. My friend Sarah (who wrote the Foreword for this book) traveled to multiple continents as an English as a Second Language (ESL) teacher, and it was an experience that forever changed the course of her life. Interested in pursuing this? More info here: teachaway.com

Become A Houseparent

If you love spending time with kids and teens, you can become a "houseparent"—a paid supervisor and live-in mentor—at a summer camp, foster care home, crisis center, treatment center, or even a private home or dormitory. Bring your big heart and lots of hugs. More over here: houseparent.net

Become A Virtual Assistant

Love noodling around with WordPress and Squarespace? Obsessed with social media nerdery? Got an eagle eye for proofreading? A knack for mastering new techie tools with ease? *Please* become a Virtual Assistant, because I have approximately three hundred past and current clients who desperately want to hire someone like you. This is not a joke. More info here: ivaa.org and here: assistu.com and here: virtualgalfriday.com

Become A Park Ranger

Prefer redwood trees to Rich Site Summary (RSS) feeds? Got an urge to clear some brush? You can apply for a seasonal or year-round position in a treasured forest—say, Yellowstone National Park in Wyoming. You'll share a dormitory with your fellow rangers and park employees, and you probably won't have cell phone service. Which sounds pretty swell to me. More here: yellowstonejobs.com

Get a Paper Route

Many years ago, while I was working to build my freelance writing portfolio, I (very briefly) worked as a magazine delivery driver to make some extra cash. (Hey, it's still the "publishing industry," right?) Insider tip: wear thick gloves, or the plastic twine will cut into your hands. Fun! But seriously, think of the stories for your memoirs! More here: wikihow.com/Get-a-Paper-Route-in-Your-Local-Community

And There's Always Yogaville...

$450 a month for room and board plus daily meditation sessions and yoga classes at YogaVille, an ashram nestled in the foothills of the Blue Ridge Mountains. As far as "back up plans" and "worse case scenarios" go, YogaVille doesn't sound too bad! More info here: yogaville.org/residential-programs/ashram-yogi-program/finances-ay/

Here's to failure, reinvention, unexpected opportunities, and the comforting knowledge that *you're going to survive*...no matter what.

Questions for Goal-Setting, Strategizing, Facing Fears, and Planning Your Next Steps.

1. What do you like about your current job or career?

2. What do you *not* like about your current job or career?

3. What kind of work would you love to be doing in the future? Describe anything that feels clear to you at this point—your ideal work environment, what kinds of colleagues you'd like to have, what types of projects you'll do, how you'd like to spend a typical workday, etc. Your *"Wow, that would be seriously amazing and wonderful"* scenario.

4. There's your current career. And then, there's the career you'd like to have in the future. What do you need to do to move from "here" to "there"?

For example—do you need a new degree? Do you need to line up some new clients? Do you need to move to New York City and get an internship at a top fashion magazine, like in *The Devil Wears Prada*? What are some steps you'll need to take?

5. For the previous question, if you're thinking, *"I have no idea what steps I need to take! Ack! I'm clueless about what to do next!"* then write down the names of some people that you could ask for guidance. Friends, family members, colleagues, people you respect and admire...anybody who might have a suggestion for you.

Write down their names. Then reach out to them, one
by one. Ask a specific question—something you're
wondering about, something you'd really love to know.
Keep it brief. Express profuse gratitude for their time. In
most instances, they'll be flattered that you trust them
and want their opinion.

6. When you think about moving towards the career that
you really want, what are some of your fears?

Are you afraid of criticism? Afraid of making an
embarrassing mistake? Afraid of being shunned by
family members who don't approve of your plans? Afraid
of wasting time, energy, or money—yours, or someone
else's? Afraid that you just don't have what it takes? All
of the above? And what else?

Write down any fears that bubble up in your mind
and heart.

7. Personally, I believe the best way to fight fear is
with *evidence*.

When I feel anxious, I gather evidence to prove to myself
that I'm smart, capable, and resourceful.

For example—I've worked with clients in the past and
(most of the time) they've been happy with my work.
That's evidence that I'm capable of working hard and
delighting my clients. I've done it before. I can do it
again. This is not a theory or a feeling. It's a *fact*.

Another example—at one point in my life, I was down
to the tiniest scrap of money. I didn't know how I was

going to make my next mortgage payment, and I was so ashamed and embarrassed. But I pulled myself together. I found a roommate, which helped out tremendously. I hustled to line up a few more projects. I sold some furniture. I also cried and almost vomited from the stress, but I did what I needed to do. I scraped together the money that I needed and I survived. That's *evidence* that I'm capable of going through a stressful time and getting myself back on my feet. I've done it before—and I can do it again. *Fact.*

What about you?

What have you survived?

What have you achieved?

What are your proudest moments?

What are the facts about your life and career?

Make a list of anything that comes to mind. Here are some prompts to get you started...

I've learned lots of skills over the course of my life/ career, including...

I've been through some difficult situations like...

I got through those situations because I...

I've created some pretty cool things over the course of my life/career, like...

I've made the world a better place by...

One thing I've achieved in the past year is...

I felt very strong that one time when I...

Looking back on my life, I'm proud of the fact that I....

I've been complimented/praised several times for my...

One thing I'm very good at is...

Even though I'm not perfect, and even though I've made mistakes in the past, I am proud of myself because...

Everything you just wrote down—that's your history. Your story. Your life. Evidence. Facts.

Read it back to youself. So many beautiful pieces of evidence. Evidence that you are smart, resourceful, capable of facing your fears and achieving your goals.

You've done plenty of things before—cool things, brave things, creative things—and you can do those kinds of things again.

So, please go forth and do the work you really want to do, whether it's accounting or astrology or practicing law or running a gourmet popsicle stand or teaching karate or starting a nonprofit educational program for kids.

Go do it. Or at least, try to do it. *Really* try. Put your full heart into it.

Remember what my friend Susan said earlier in this book?

"When you make a full-hearted effort, you get full-sized results."

***

Phone Numbers, Websites, and Resources.

Feeling isolated? Feeling bored? Feel like you don't have any friends who support your personal and professional goals? Feel like you're marching all alone?

Head to **MEETUP.COM.** Search to find a group that excites you. Maybe a writing group. Or a hiking group. Or a small business owners group. Or a brunch group.

There are over twenty-two million Meetup members in 180 countries and over two hundred thousand groups that meet regularly. Whatever you're into, you can find people who are into that, too.

Don't see the type of group you want to join? Seize the initiative and start it yourself!

***

Trying to start a business? Feeling overwhelmed and discouraged?

Head to **SCORE.ORG** to find a business mentor in your city. You can get mentored...for *free*. Yup. There are kind, caring, seasoned entrepreneurs who want to give you advice and encouragement—at no cost. Yes, really.

***

Having a really hard time in your life—or career? Feel like nothing's ever going to get better? Feel like the world would be better off without you?

Please go to **SUICIDEPREVENTIONLIFELINE. ORG**. Or call **1-800-273-8255**. Or go to **CRISISTEXTLINE.ORG**.

There are volunteers who are standing by, ready to talk to you or text with you 24/7. There are people who are willing to hear *anything* you need to say, no matter how messy, shameful, or crazy you think it sounds. There are people who have felt what you're feeling. There are people who want to help you find a reason to live. Please reach out to them.

Even if you're not feeling suicidal—just anxious and upset—it's OK to reach out to the National Suicide Prevention Lifeline. Do it. There's no cost, and the Lifeline volunteers would be so happy to support you.

Get a Free Pep Talk.

Do you need a pep talk? Are you struggling with difficult time in your career, feeling anxious about the future, or just feeling stuck, tired, overwhelmed, or unmotivated?

If you want, you can send an email to **hello@ alexandrafranzen.com** and say:

"Hi. I could really use a pep talk."

I will send an encouraging pep talk (audio recording) back to you. It might take me a few days, or even a week, so please be patient. I will reply as soon as I can. I hope it boosts your spirits, even just a tiny bit.

It's free. It's my pleasure. This is not a trick, or a joke, and there's no catch. It's for real. So reach out if you want to.

A Few Final Thoughts

You Can Do Hard Things.

Right around her thirtieth birthday, my friend Nicole decided to complete a 460-mile hike through the wilderness. Alone.

She'd never done anything like this before. A city girl who's lived in Los Angeles, New York City, and London, her "outdoor survival experience" was limited to sipping iced tea on a patio in downtown LA. But something burned inside of her belly. She was determined to embark on this adventure—to prove to herself that she could conquer this challenge. She spent hundreds of hours Googling, researching, and reading books on hiking, trekking, and how to avoid getting eaten by bears. She taught herself how to read a map. She practiced setting up a tent a few times. She figured she could handle it. And she did it.

After completing the 460th mile, she went home to her husband and cats and—of course—she got flooded with texts, emails, and phone calls from friends. Like me.

I wanted to know, "How did it go? How do you feel?"

She told me:

"It was beautiful and it was awful. My feet were blistered the entire time. I collapsed and cried and I almost gave up a hundred different times. But I wanted to prove to myself that I can be the type of person who finishes what she starts. I've always quit on myself in the past, but this time, I promised myself it would be different. So I finished the hike. And I felt so much joy. And I can't wait to do it again."

She also said to me:

"You know, as human beings, we're so afraid of discomfort, even temporary discomfort. We're so afraid of challenges. We're so afraid of anything that feels 'hard.' But we can do hard things. Our bodies, our minds, our spirits…we are designed to do hard things."

For days, I kept hearing Nicole's words echoing in my mind.

We can do hard things.

She's right. We can endure temporary discomfort. It's what we're designed to do. Physical discomfort—like hiking 460 miles across the rugged wilderness with a heavy pack on your shoulders. Emotional discomfort— like applying for your dream job and then dealing with uncertainty, not knowing if you'll be selected or rejected. Other types of emotional discomfort, too—like releasing your latest song, product, or book, and then dealing with snarky comments, low sales, or no sales at all, not the wildly positive reception you hoped to receive.

As Nicole reminded me, we are designed to do hard things, and we are designed to handle all of life's difficulties. Not only that, but doing hard stuff can feel really amazing. Meaningful. Important. Satisfying. Life-altering. Even joyful.

Maybe this is why we challenge ourselves mentally, physically, and creatively. It's not just for applause. It's not for Amazon reviews. It's not for comments, likes, and Instagram hearts. It's because we want to feel *intense joy*—not the fleeting dopamine burst of a re-tweet, but deep, powerful joy. It's because we want to feel proud of ourselves. Because we want to feel strong and capable. Because we want to feel alive. Because we want to make things and do things, and leave a mark on the world to say...

"I was here."

In my experience, the projects, goals, and endeavors that bring that incredible feeling—*"I was here." "I matter." "I'm alive."*—typically aren't the endeavors that bring immediate gratification.

The gratification comes later. You wait for it. You earn it. It's hard, courageous work. And it's worth it.

* * *

Discouragement Never Really Ends.

Newbie writers and entrepreneurs sometimes ask me, "Alex, how does it feel now that you've got plenty of clients, now that you've had books published, you know...now that you've 'made it'?"

Now that I've "made it"? Uh, I don't feel like I've ever really "made it." And also, it feels...just as terrifying as it did ten years ago when I was trying to get my very first article published.

Everything is still scary—just in different ways. Instead of worrying about paying my rent, I worry about disappointing my clients, or disappointing my publisher with low book sales. Instead of worrying if anybody's going to read my latest blog post, I worried about getting plagiarized, misquoted, or pummeled with Internet hate mail. Instead of worrying that nobody's noticing me, I worry that too many people are noticing me—and maybe they're gossiping about me or writing terrible reviews about my projects.

Criticism. Rejection. Discouragement. Difficult moments. Setbacks. Creative blocks.

This stuff never really "stops."

First-year interns face discouraging moments, and so do A-list actors and bestselling authors and presidential nominees.

Discouragement has no expiration date.

It's one of those unavoidable emotions that we all have to face at some point or another.

And if you've chosen a "creative" or an "unconventional" career, congratulations! Buckle up, because you're in for triple the usual amount of discouragement. It's all part of the path that you've chosen. You can't run or hide from it. You've just got to embrace it.

* * *

Please Don't Give Up.

Discouragement is unavoidable. You're definitely going to feel it. And feel it. And feel it. But please don't let it crush your spirit. Please don't give up. Please don't stop trying. Please don't stop making your art, whatever it may be.

Because the worst thing—far worse that any temporary moment of discouragement—is stuffing your big dream in a box and giving up forever. That feels worse than anything. That feels like...breaking your own heart. Please don't do that.

You've got to do whatever type of work makes you feel happy and alive, because this is your one and only life.

* * *

Pain Can Harden You and Make You Bitter, or...Make You Smarter, Funnier, More Compassionate, and More Interesting.

It might not always seem like it, but I firmly believe that all of the challenges you face will shape you into a better artist—and a better human being—with even more to say and share.

Nobody ever wrote a Pulitzer Prize-winning memoir about a perfect life with zero challenges, you know?

Pain can make you smarter, funnier, more compassionate and more interesting.

Rejection can test your faith and help you decide, "Do I really want this or not?"

Criticism can unlock the greatest idea you've ever had.

All of these uncomfortable emotions and experiences—it's all fuel for your career. It's all fodder for your next book. It's all valuable and useful—if you decide to see it that way.

* * *

You're Going To Make It Through This Day.

No matter what's happening in your career right now, and no matter what happens next, you're going to make it through this day.

You were built to handle all of the challenges you're currently facing, and more.

You're made of carbon, just like the stars in the galaxy, and oxygen, hydrogen, and sodium, just like the oceans, and you're just as powerful.

You're going to survive.

Share Your Own Survival Story

You've been through difficult stuff. We all have.

It's so important to share our Survival Stories publicly. We don't do this enough.

No pressure, but...if you feel like it, I encourage you to talk about your struggles, your frustrations, your most discouraging moments, and what you've learned. Don't keep these things a secret.

The next time you're sitting down for dinner with your family, or writing a blog post, or getting onstage, or trying to motivate your team at work, why not tell that story about...

—The worst job interview you can remember.

—That time you screwed up at work and really disappointed your boss.

—That time you felt harshly criticized and it really hurt your feelings.

—How you felt when you started your business and you had almost zero clients.

—Getting bullied, betrayed, or mistreated in some way.

—A time when you felt convinced you'd get hired—but you didn't.

—A time when you felt lost, confused, and purposeless.

—A time when you felt like your work didn't really "matter."

—Or any other any story that comes to mind.

You can say:

"This is what happened to me...This is how it felt...And this is what I learned."

Extra credit: Imagine someone out there is struggling with something really similar, and they're feeling so tired, so anxious, so freaked out, or really ashamed and alone. What do you want that person to know?

You can conclude your story by saying:

"If you're ever dealing with something similar, here's my advice..." Or *"Here's what I wish I'd known back then..."*

When you share a Survival Story, it's a really brave thing to do. It can lead to amazing discussions around the dinner table, and deeper friendships, and deeper connections with your blog readers, clients, or customers, and...who knows? By sharing your story, you might inspire someone to start a new business, pursue their dream job, or continue to work on a big goal instead of giving up.

You might feel kinda nervous to share your story. You might think to yourself, *"Oh, nobody wants to hear my dumb story. It's not that interesting."* or, *"People will think I'm 'unprofessional' or 'too emotional'. I probably shouldn't say this."*

Well, no. That's incorrect. People *do* want to hear your story. People are always fascinated to hear about other people's struggles, mistakes, and most difficult moments.

Your story could change someone's whole day—or life.
So, you should probably tell it.

I hope that you will.

Gratitude

Creating this book required a lot of people's time, energy, brains, and typing fingers.

I need to give a huge, epic *thank you* to…

—Everyone who contributed a Survival Story for this book, and said, *"Hey, it's cool, I don't mind if you interview me and then publish one of the worst experiences of my entire life."*

Here they are, in alphabetical order! Please visit their websites, buy their books, buy their albums, go to their concerts, sign up for their programs, send them fan mail, and shower them with appreciation!

Ben Wendel

- https://benwendel.com/

Brandon Weeks

- http://hunnymilk.com/

Dale Franzen

- http://hadestown.com/

Ellen Fondiler

- http://ellenfondiler.com/

L'Erin Alta

- http://lerinalta.com/

Maggie Reyes

- http://modernmarried.com/

Maria Ross

- http://red-slice.com/

Melinda Massie

- https://asideoffab.com/

Melissa Cassera

- http://melissacassera.com/

Niki Driscoll

- http://nikidriscoll.com/

Paul Jarvis

- https://pjrvs.com/

Robert Hartwell

- http://bwaycollective.com/

Shauna Haider

- http://nubbytwiglet.com/

- http://wearebranch.com/

Shelley Cohen

- https://fromshelleywithlove.com

Susan Hyatt and her daughter Emily

(Note: Emily sometimes goes by "Cora")

- https://shyatt.com/

- https://facebook.com/wenchtheatrecompany/

Theresa Reed

- http://thetarotlady.com/

Also, special thanks to...

Jeff Nelson

- http://yoxo.com/

Justin Thomas

- instagram.com/dinosaur.knuckles/

Master Phil Nguyen

- http://blackbeltexcellence.com/

Nicole Antoinette

- https://nicoleantoinette.com/

...for being part of my life, and for inspiring me to be braver and stronger in every way.

I also need to say *thank you* to...

—Sarah Von Bargen, my sweet, dear friend, for contributing a Foreword for this book, and for saying "Yes" to a coffee date with a complete stranger from the Internet (me!) all those years ago. I just want to fly to Vegas and eat crispy potato shoestring hash browns and hollandaise sauce with you for all of time.

—Woz Flint and Cher Hale for proofreading this book so carefully and discovering all of my stray commas and typos and other horrendous problems.

—Brenda Knight at Mango Publishing for saying "Yes" to this project after twenty other publishers and literary agents said "No, thank you."

—Colleen Martell and Stephanie Tade from the Tade Literary Agency for your wonderful, smart, helpful ideas on how to make this book better. Even though you ultimately told me, "We can't represent you," you were so amazingly nice about it. Thanks for that.

—My local Starbucks baristas for fueling me with endless coffee and for always asking, "What are you working on today?" and "How's the book coming along?"

—All of my clients, blog readers, newsletter subscribers, and other members of my Internet family. Many of you have followed my work for six, seven, eight years or more, and you've seen me morph through countless personal evolutions, business models, hairstyles, and all kinds of creative projects. As you've watched from afar, I've found my voice, and I've stumbled into the messages that I really want to talk about and share. Whether we've ever met in "real life" or not, I'm grateful for your presence in my life.

—Even though we'll probably never meet in real life, I also want to thank...David Wagner, the founder of The Daymaker Movement. RuPaul, my chosen spiritual leader. The Dalai Lama. David Blaine, because your artistry inspires me tremendously. And Michelle Obama, because...of too many reasons to list.

—And of course, I need to thank my parents. Dad, you taught me how to be patient and compassionate, even when it's not easy to do so. Mom, you told me that I was going to grow up and become a writer, and even though I resisted that path for a while, turns out you were right. (As usual. Ugh, mom, why are you always right?)

—Ben and Olivia, my crazy siblings (and I mean "crazy" as a compliment, of course). You make me laugh harder than anybody else in the world.

—And last but not least: Brandon. Thank you for being the best partner I could possibly imagine. Thank you for listening to me talk endlessly about the books and other projects I want to create. Thank you for reminding me to eat and bathe and pop outside into the fresh air instead of typing 24/7. Thank you for helping me evolve into the best version of myself. You're so good to me, and so good for me. I love you foreverly.

About The Author

Alexandra Franzen is a writer based in Portland, Oregon.

She has written two nonfiction books, two self-published novels, and hundreds of articles and essays. Her writing has been featured in places like *Time*, *Forbes*, *Newsweek*, *The Huffington Post*, and *Lifehacker*. She has been mentioned in places like *You're The Boss! The New York Times Small Business Blog*, *The Atlantic*, and *Inc.*

She primarily writes about creativity, productivity, communication, goal-setting, and how to deal with adversity in your life and career—negative reviews, projects that don't pan out, all kinds of painful moments that can rattle your self-esteem—and how to keep marching forward, no matter what.

As a ghostwriter, copywriter, and communication consultant, Alexandra has worked with tech companies like Hewlett-Packard, celebrity-driven brands like Rachel Zoe's DreamDry, fitness companies like Curvy Yoga, and over one hundred public speakers, authors, artists, and entrepreneurs. She also leads classes and retreats for people who want to work on books, blogs, podcasts, and other creative projects.

You can learn more about Alexandra's projects at: **AlexandraFranzen.com**

You can send messages (nice ones, hopefully?) to: **hello@alexandrafranzen.com**

Thank You For Reading.

You're Going To Survive.

You're Stronger Than You Think.

And...

Today Is Not Over Yet.